Legacy to Leadership – The roadmap from employee to entrepreneur

Verses Kindler Publication

Verses Kindler Publication.

Website: www.verseskindlerpublication.com

Legacy to Leadership - The roadmap from employee to entrepreneur

By: Mr. Ravi Shanker Ukrani

ISBN: **978-93-49532-79-3**

1st Edition

Price: INR 449/$20

Disclaimer

Legacy to Leadership - The roadmap from employee to entrepreneur is authored by Ravi Shanker Ukrani. The entirety of this published work comprises the original content of the author, who has undertaken diligent efforts in its editing. The characters depicted herein may be fictitious or inspired by real events; however, they are not intended to cause offense or represent any prejudice against any caste or system. Any similarity to the names of actual individuals, locations, or institutions is purely coincidental and serves the narrative. The author bears sole responsibility for the originality of this work; the publisher assumes no liability thereof.

Dedication

To the visionaries - those who dream boldly and act with courage. May this book serve as both inspiration and fuel for your journey.

To my parents and family, whose unwavering support have shaped who I am today.

And to my dear friend— whose steadfast presence and support have been a lighthouse in every storm. Thank you for standing by me, always.

Index

Introduction: The Entrepreneur's Compass

Entrepreneurship is not skills or knowledge—it's an attitude that inspires, directs, and determines how issues are approached. It's characterised by the capacity to envision opportunities others perceive as hindrances, the capacity to create worth from what might be limited resources and openness to risk with the premise that even failure is part of the journey to success.

Here, you'll discover how to foster an entrepreneurial mindset that will support you through the transition from employee to thriving entrepreneur. This mindset is crucial whether developing a side hustle or the complete transition to business ownership. It will get you moving from a place of security into a place of promise, where every obstacle is an opportunity for innovation and expansion.

1. Your Employee-to-Entrepreneur Transition:

Most of us conceptualise entrepreneurship as a forte of the wealthy, someone with plenty of funds and unique expertise. That is wrong, though. Entrepreneurship is a mindset that can be learned based on upbringing and existing job descriptions. Being an entrepreneur is not about giving up your established job; it is about adopting a different attitude, behaviour, and manner of interacting with the world.

Along the way, we'll show you how many successful people have figured out how to outsmart those internal and external barriers and how to play to your strengths, many of which you've already learned working as an employee. You will learn to take charge, innovate, and operate with risk, developing the confidence you need to seize opportunities.

By the end of this journey, you'll have a clear roadmap to turn your entrepreneurial dreams into reality, with a mindset primed for success.

2. How an Entrepreneurial Mindset Will Enable You To Reframe Issues And Opportunities:

An entrepreneurial mindset is a supervision that will help you see obstacles from a new perspective. Where other people see barrier and notice limitations, entrepreneurs see possibilities and opportunities to develop something else, approach a transition, or improve.

Think of an instance or an issue at your current workplace. There could be a gap within a process or the services offered. As an employee, you'd wait for directions or seek help from others to fix it. But as an entrepreneur, you'd turn solutions around within yourself, test and try another way, and use the space to innovate. Even if you fail in your entrepreneurial venture, the mindset to try and learn something new from each endeavour is what entrepreneurs are known for.

This mindset shift—failure not being a hindrance but a stepping stone—can enable you to see opportunities that others may not.

It is about becoming more resourceful, thinking critically, and capable of doing something worthwhile.

Defining the Entrepreneurial Mindset

1. Initiative: Doing Without Being Told To:

The initiative is the most entrepreneurial trait. It's doing without being told to, seeing opportunities, and taking them without being asked. Workers wait to be told what to do, but entrepreneurs take charge. They don't sit around waiting for luck to knock on the door; instead, they create the door and push it open.

Take the case of Elon Musk, who never sought to settle in the space market but proceeded and established SpaceX amidst existing giants in this field, NASA and Boeing. His enthusiasm, driven by his passion for space and newness, enabled newer technologies to be incorporated and made available for anyone to explore space. Entrepreneurially oriented-people like him never seek when to begin but do and make things happen.

To you, the initiative will be about being smart, seeing where you can improve your business or work concepts, and acting on them. It's a question of breaking the passive thinking that far too often pervades the old job culture and stepping into a proactive arena where you take personal responsibility to make things happen.

2. Innovation: Thinking Creatively to Solve Problems:

Entrepreneurship is all about innovation. Innovation means thinking creatively to repair something or build something new. An entrepreneur's mind lives on reinventing and making things better day by day. Employees are worried about getting the job done as fast as possible, but entrepreneurs are interested in how they can repair or break systems.

Take Steve Jobs and Apple as a case in point. Jobs didn't just build products to fulfil demand; he built and shaped demand. The iPhone revolutionised how individuals communicated. Jobs' philosophy reshaped industries and formed new ones, breaking conventions of possibility.

To you, innovation may not mean creating a revolutionary product to sell. It can be as easy as inventing new ways of delivering value, streamlining processes, or simply doing something the competition isn't. Innovation is being curious, open, and boundary-pushing.

3. Risk-taking: Managing Risk and Uncertainty:

The third of the entrepreneurial mindset's core areas is risk-taking. Entrepreneurs don't avoid risk—they know how to manage it. Entrepreneurship is about managing uncertainty, whether launching a new product, venturing into a new market, or trying a new business. It is not an irresponsible risk but a smart risk when making well-thought-out decisions.

Consider, for instance, Richard Branson, the entrepreneur behind Virgin Group. Branson has made gigantic bets, i.e., attempting to enter the airline and communications business, that all attempts could have easily failed. But he survived the gambles because he believed in his instincts, researched, and was flexible enough to emerge as one of the world's finest entrepreneurs. He was not discouraged from trying because he feared failure; risk was a way of advancement.

To you, the risk is confronting the unknown. It is about assessing the risks but refusing to let them immobilise you. Being an entrepreneur is all about making sound decisions, moving forward in fear, and being ready to spring into action when things do not turn out right.

Why Employees Make Great Entrepreneurs

1. Industry Experience: Understanding of Market Conditions and Consumer Needs

Employees most frequently have one clear edge as entrepreneurs: superior industry experience in the business segment they are working in. Industry experience provides feedback regarding customer challenges, market conditions, and competitive landscapes. New entrepreneurs must spend time acquainting themselves with the market, whereas employees have insider knowledge concerning problems and potential within their industry. They recognise customers' issues and can see areas of gap in the market where there's a void for innovation.

Imagine, for instance, the case of Jeff Bezos, the owner of Amazon. Before starting Amazon, Bezos had also been employed on Wall

Street, where he could envision the potential of buying and selling online and expanding the Internet business to a broader scale. As he had already worked there, he could foresee the enormous shift to e-commerce and make Amazon a trendsetter when the company was nascent. His profound understanding of the company and the customers' needs propelled Amazon from a small online bookstore to one of the world's most influential institutions.

Experience is a strong asset for future entrepreneurs already working in an industry. They already know what they can and cannot do and how to address customers' pain points, a benefit that most entrepreneurs don't have when entering a new industry.

2. Discipline: Work under Pressure, Work to Deadlines, and Manage Responsibilities:

Discipline is the most essential quality employees gain while transforming from corporate life to entrepreneurship. Corporate life exposes employees to working under deadlines, work balance, and delivering results within planned time limits. All these activities help one possess a good work culture, stress management capability, and under-pressure organisational capability—all for enterprise success.

Take the example of Howard Schultz, former CEO of Starbucks. Before revolutionising Starbucks into the global coffee giant we know, Schultz worked as the Director of Retail Operations and Marketing for a small coffee company. Schultz's hands-on experience managing multiple stores, maintaining the pace of operations, and functioning within tight deadlines helped him learn how to create a scalable business model. His prudence and steadfastness helped him turn Starbucks into a global giant.

Entrepreneurs who have tasted the benefits of working in a structured environment have already developed the self-discipline to manage time, handle multiple tasks, and implement plans under pressure. Such skills are invaluable when they eventually start and run their businesses.

3. Professional Networks: Colleague, Mentor, and Industry Influencer Relationships

One of the least appreciated advantages employees enjoy when venturing into entrepreneurship is their professional network. Employees learn from colleagues and mentors and establish connections with different clients and other industry players. These professionals offer guidance, information, and assistance while venturing into entrepreneurship.

For example, Facebook cofounder Mark Zuckerberg leveraged his network at Harvard to obtain the initial funding and support needed to create Facebook. Eduardo Saverin, who roomed with Zuckerberg, was central to Facebook's initial funding, and other initial connections helped the firm get airborne. Zuckerberg's network was key in getting Facebook off the ground, from obtaining investment to promoting the site.

As an employee, you have already built a network to tap into when you start your business. Your network can be a valuable friend when you start as an entrepreneur, whether you need advice, money, or partnering with industry contacts.

The Mindset Shift: From Job Security to Creating Opportunities

1. Uncertainty Phobia: How to Overcome Fear of Moving Beyond Job Security

Fear of uncertainty ranks among the most formidable psychological barriers to transitioning from employee to entrepreneur. As an employee, you have a steady paycheck, a specific environment, and some degree of job security. When making the entrepreneurial jump, this security vanishes, replaced by the unpredictabilities of entrepreneurship and running and starting a company. The fear of failure, financial insecurity, and the stress of decision-making can be overwhelming.

But this fear can be moderated. The secret is to embrace uncertainty as an accompaniment to the entrepreneurial journey. Rather than feeling it's a minus, see it as an opportunity to learn, evolve, and innovate. Successful entrepreneurs don't eliminate uncertainty; they learn to manage it. Acknowledge your fears, but don't allow them to rule you. Instead, develop a risk management strategy and start small to get a toe in before jumping in full.

For example, Spanx founder Sarah Blakely used her savings to start her venture. Although the road ahead was uncertain, she faced her fears and believed in her doggedness and faith in what she had created. Blakely took calculated gambles and used her initial doubt as a push factor to carry on.

2. Proactive Mindset: Shifting from a Reactive Task-Oriented Mindset to One of Creating Value and Seizing Opportunities

One of the most significant shifts you go through when switching from being an employee to becoming an entrepreneur is shifting from a reactive task-oriented mindset to creating value. When you are an employee, your maximum efforts go into getting the job done and accomplishing deadlines. Others tell you what structure and direction to take. But as an entrepreneur, you set the goals and the tasks necessary. Your mindset must be from just accomplishing tasks to creating opportunities and solutions.

Entrepreneurs do not wait for things to happen—they make them happen. Proactivity involves anticipating, setting goals clearly, and taking actions that propel the business forward. For instance, Bill Gates and Paul Allen, Microsoft co-founders, did not wait for the software industry to emerge—they envisioned and created a business model that revolutionised personal computing.

To develop this attitude, start by examining your current activities and asking yourself, "What could I do differently?" or "How could I transform this process?" Moving from a passive to an active mindset will help you take control of your entrepreneurial path.

3. Embracing Risk: Transitioning from Seeking Stability to Embracing the Inherent Uncertainties of Entrepreneurship

Entrepreneurship is inherently risky. Moving away from the security of a traditional job means navigating ambiguity, market fluctuations, and possible failure. The key to thriving in entrepreneurship is embracing risk, not avoiding it. It's essential to recognise that risk doesn't mean recklessness—it means taking informed risks with the potential for high rewards.

Warren Buffett, known for his calculated risk-taking in investments, once said, "Risk comes from not knowing what you're doing." Successful entrepreneurs understand how to manage risk by conducting thorough research, testing their ideas in small ways, and staying flexible.

To adapt to this change, start by redefining your attitude towards risk. Instead of viewing it as an object of fear, view it as an opportunity to develop and learn. Little changes, like test-running your business concept on a small scale or seeking guidance, can help you build the confidence required to take more significant risks in the future.

4. Some Practical Tips for Succeeding with This Transition

Start Small: Pilot your business while you continue to work. This reduces risk and gives you time to learn.

- Establish Clear Goals: Short-term goals will help you successfully transition from employee to entrepreneur.

- Find Mentorship: Find a mentor or join entrepreneurial networks to gain knowledge and be guided through the transition.
- Build a Financial Safety Net: Save first before taking the plunge. Financial cushions take the fear out of walking away from a steady income.

Overview of the Book and What You Will Gain

This book is designed to guide you on your journey from employee to entrepreneur. Each chapter is carefully planned to assist you in developing the mindset, skills, and knowledge required to be successful. From discovering the core traits of entrepreneurs to practical advice on launching your own business, you will possess all you need to begin your entrepreneurial journey confidently.

Key Takeaways and Insights: Throughout the book, you'll find key insights and actionable steps to take you along the way. These are the key things that will empower you enough to make that successful transition from employee to entrepreneur:

Practical Strategies and Tools: Each chapter will include step-by-step advice to help you apply the concepts discussed. These will be action plans, strategies for setting goals, and case studies to demonstrate how others have effectively made the shift.

Mindset Development: This book focuses on building and maintaining an entrepreneurial mindset. You'll learn to stay focused, overcome self-doubt, and cultivate the mental fortitude to keep moving forward, even in challenging times.

Case Studies and Real-World Examples: Throughout the book, you'll encounter stories of successful entrepreneurs who started as employees. These case studies demonstrate how they successfully leveraged their experiences, skills, and networks to transition to entrepreneurship.

Actionable Exercises: Each chapter will conclude with self-assessment exercises and planning aids that you will employ to implement the learnings in your own life. The exercises help you gauge your entrepreneurial readiness, identify your strengths, and craft a clear action plan to propel you forward.

By the end of this book, you'll have the tools to overcome obstacles like fear and uncertainty. You'll learn to leverage your existing skills, knowledge, and networks to fuel your entrepreneurial journey. Entrepreneurship takes time, but with the right approach and mindset, you'll be ready to build your business.

You'll be equipped to pursue your entrepreneurial dreams with the skills and confidence to create opportunities that align with your values.

Conclusion:

You've learned how adopting an entrepreneurial mindset can help you transition from employee to entrepreneur. Your work experience—industry knowledge, discipline, and connections—can be a strong foundation for starting your business. The path to entrepreneurship involves cultivating a new mindset, creating opportunities, and managing risks.

In **Chapter 1: Unlocking the Entrepreneur Within**, we'll explore core entrepreneurial principles, traits of successful entrepreneurs, and how to develop these traits yourself. By the end, you'll have the tools to assess your preparedness and areas for growth.

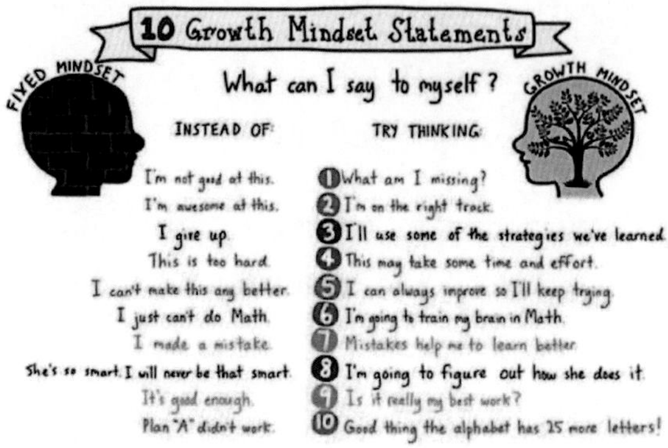

Chapter 1: Unlocking the Entrepreneur Within

Hello, and so starts the process of becoming the entrepreneur inside you. This chapter is a huge stepping stone towards understanding what it takes to be an entrepreneur and how, as an employee yourself, you can be one, too. It's not necessarily about a business idea but rather gearing up the mindset and skills that will get you through.

Here, we are going to discuss what an entrepreneur is. We will elaborate on the most essential characteristics of successful business persons, i.e., risk-taking ability, creativity, flexibility, and perseverance. These qualities distinguish business persons from all other people, and once you know them, you will be conscious of how to develop such qualities in you. We will also tackle some of the most prevalent myths about entrepreneurship and shatter myths such as "entrepreneurs are born, not made" and "you need lots of money to be an entrepreneur."

Lastly, we will guide you through an exercise of self-appraisal, where you examine your weaknesses and strengths. Your appraisal will serve as the foundation upon which the rest of this book will be built so that you can determine whether you are entrepreneurial-ready and what you need to do.

At the end of this chapter, you should understand what it's like to be an entrepreneur and why it's more a question of attitude and approach than simply owning a company. You'll see that entrepreneurship isn't a recipe; it is just a constant process anyone can master with the right attitude and equipment.

This chapter will also provide some perspective on why so many of you, your employees, and others like you can be entrepreneurs. You'll see that entrepreneurship is not a question of waiting for the right time or that flash-of-genius thought. It's a matter of doing better, making things better, creating value, and handling the uncertainty of entrepreneurship.

What It Means to Be an Entrepreneur

A Comprehensive Definition of Entrepreneurship:

Essentially, entrepreneurship is the skill of doing something new: business, product, service, or idea—that meets a need or solves a problem one identifies. Entrepreneurship is the art of recognising something nobody else does and being bold enough to make it real. Innovation, risk-taking, and value creation are the recipe for entrepreneurial success as a profession.

Innovation is entrepreneurship. Entrepreneurs don't start companies—they invent new things, improve existing ways of doing things, and disrupt industries. Innovation can be incremental or high-impact, radical or marginal, but it always leads to a better, simpler, or more efficient life.

Value creation is just good entrepreneurship. Entrepreneurs are not dispensers of cash; they are individuals who want to create value and fix customer problems. Entrepreneurs do a good job of building value in the customers' lives.

Independence is the second most crucial entrepreneurial quality. Entrepreneurs are not dependent; they do not seek somebody else's advice or leave the direction of their actions and decisions in somebody else's hands. They decide their purpose, set their course, and are responsible for the outcome of their enterprise as well.

Entrepreneurship is not business ownership but an attitude of working full-time to generate value. The following are the three most critical principles which any entrepreneur needs to adopt:

- Creating Value: Entrepreneurs are problem-solvers. By producing a product, service, or solution, entrepreneurs learn what the marketplace requires and deliver improved products that satisfy them. Value creation lies at the heart of each successful entrepreneurial venture.

- Problem-Solving: A company exists only to solve a problem. Successful business people earn their living by finding the customer's pain, sensing the customer's need, and inventing new solutions that better satisfy the need than the alternative.
- Being Self-Directed: Entrepreneurs are self-directed. They do not wait for someone to guide them; they guide themselves. Self-directed is being proactive, taking the initiative, and driving the business forward when uncertain or complex.

Examples of Entrepreneurs Who Possess These Traits

Elon Musk is a well-known, value-creating, innovative entrepreneur. He created innovation in every field of the car industry, including electric cars (Tesla) and space tourism (SpaceX), by finding gaps in terrestrial transportation and space travel and filling them with value innovation fillers.

Another fantastic value-creator entrepreneur is Oprah Winfrey. She established her media empire by figuring out what the audience requires, delivering the requirements in the form of compelling content, and establishing a new mechanism for delivering media. It was less about creating a business and more about creating a culture that delivered unparalleled value to human lives.

Sara Blakely, the founder of Spanx, is as quintessential a problem-solver-entrepreneur as they come. She began with a humble idea, found that there wasn't high-end shapewear anywhere, and proceeded to build a billion-dollar brand. She powered it by understanding what women needed, having an unconventional solution for the product, and a necessity to solve something prevalent on all continents of the globe.

Entrepreneurship is less about starting a business and more about developing core skills that allow you to bounce back from failure, think creatively, be flexible, and sustain growth. Successful entrepreneurs will likely be resilient, creative, flexible, and risk-takers. Let's define each of these characteristics:

Resilience: The Ability to Bounce Back from Failure

Resilience is an essential attribute of any entrepreneur. Entrepreneurial existence is complete with failure, setbacks, and adversity. Resilience allows entrepreneurs to persist in the face of adversity, learn from failure, and fail to get enraged in the face of adversity. Without resilience, one would lose hope ahead of failure or setbacks, but successful entrepreneurs employ failure as a stepping stone.

For example, Steve Jobs is the very definition of resilience. Ousted by the firm he had created, Apple, Jobs did not let failure get the better of him. Instead, he left and created NeXT and bought Pixar, the start of one of the greatest business comebacks ever. Jobs re-energized Apple and made it the world's biggest company, bearing witness to the fact that failure, with determination, can be the launching pad for success.

Key Takeaway: Great entrepreneurs do not equate failure as an endpoint but a launching point to knowledge. Failure is the time to learn, the time to recalculate, and the time to be better.

Creativity: Thinking beyond the ordinary Outside the Box

Creativity is the capacity to see different and problem-solving solutions that other individuals do not see. Innovators personify creativity through product innovation, re-creating the known or bridging the gap with the knowledge that the customers lack. Creativity can make the difference between successful entrepreneurs and others, enabling them to craft businesses that become iconic brands in competitive industries.

Key Takeaway: Entrepreneurs apply imagination to address challenges in innovative and nontraditional ways, enabling possible value that resonates with customers and keeps up with the competition.

Adaptability: Staying Agile in an Evolving Business World

Adaptability is the ability to change and modify one's approach in response to changes in the business environment, market forces, or client demands. Business is constantly evolving, and business people must be capable of adapting to such changes to stay updated. Flexible entrepreneurs can redirect when needed and exploit new opportunities that arise.

Example: Jeff Bezos is the best example of flexibility. Amazon started as an online bookshop, but shortly after, Bezos remodelled the business to sell more products as the market shifted. Bezos' ability to modify the business based on consumer trends, technological innovations, and competition has been the momentum behind Amazon's magnitude.

Key Takeaway: Entrepreneurs who capitalise on flexibility can stay ahead of the curve and turn challenges into opportunities by being responsive and adaptable to change.

Risk-Taking: Strategic Risk-Taking as a Business Growth Element

Entrepreneurship carries inherent risks—financial, personal, and professional. But successful entrepreneurs are not reckless; they're calculating risk-takers who balance potential rewards and consequences. They make informed decisions based on facts, intuition, and experience, risking possible benefits. The secret here is that risk-taking in business is wise decision-making, not blind faith.

For instance, Virgin Group creator Richard Branson has a knack for being a risk-taker. From beginning Virgin Records to developing Virgin Atlantic Airways, again and again, Branson created risks and tasks for his reward. However, research, careful planning, and market studies have preceded the taking of those risks. Branson is the paradigm of how meticulous planning, consideration, and background studies can yield monumental business successes through calculated risks.

Key Takeaway: Risk is inherent in entrepreneurship, but effective entrepreneurs know how to contain risk by preparing well and making good decisions. Taking risks allows entrepreneurs to access new opportunities and grow their businesses.

Misconceptions About Entrepreneurship

Entrepreneurship is widely misconceived, fueled by myths and assumptions discouraging most individuals from trying it. Debunking such myths is essential to enlighten readers on entrepreneurship's real face. Here, we shall address three of the most common myths.

"Entrepreneurs Are Born, Not Made."

One of the most prevalent myths about entrepreneurship is that entrepreneurs are born with certain qualities and traits that others lack. Successful entrepreneurs, this myth states, have inherent attributes—vision, charisma, or risk tolerance—that cannot be learned or acquired.

The truth is that entrepreneurship is a set of skills that anybody can learn. Although some characteristics, like resilience or creativity, may come more naturally to specific individuals, all these characteristics can be acquired and refined by practice, reading, and exposure. Most successful entrepreneurs did not have the business gene at birth. Instead, they worked incredibly hard to develop their entrepreneurial skills and mindset.

Example: Sara Blakely, the founder of Spanx, is the quintessential example of an entrepreneur who was not business-minded by birth. She started with little fashion or business acumen and utilised persistence, learning, and failure to develop a billion-dollar enterprise.

Counterargument: Anyone can be an entrepreneur by gaining the appropriate mindset, skills, and approach through learning, abilities, and tactics, regardless of background or innateness.

"You Need a Lot of Money to Start."

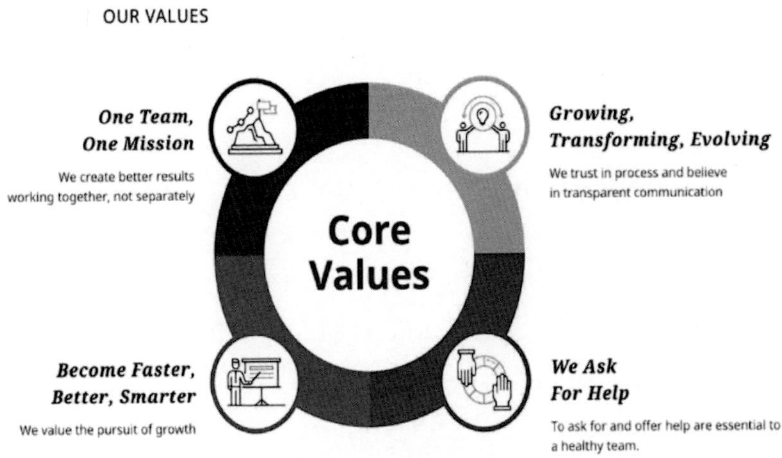

Another myth is that entrepreneurship requires a lot of money, or you must have a tremendous amount to begin. While having money available can simplify things, many entrepreneurs have started successful companies with little or no starting capital. The secret is to start small, be conservative, and focus on creating value with less capital.

For example, Starbucks' founder, Howard Schultz, started with little money. He did not have a big budget to launch Starbucks but utilised creativity, marketing skills, and vision to establish the business as a global name.

Counterargument:

Successful entrepreneurs start with little capital but utilise creativity, resourcefulness, and small-scale operations to pilot-test their business concepts before scaling.

Most individuals believe that entrepreneurship revolves around possessing an idea that will change the world. Great ideas certainly matter, yet entrepreneurship is not so much about ideas as it is about implementation, perseverance, and the ability to fix things creatively. It's more about making the concept work and creating value than possessing an idea.

For example, Mark Zuckerberg did not create social media, but he did develop Facebook. This platform improved upon the existing social networks and expanded the definition of socialising online in ways never before attempted. His achievement was not based on a world-changing concept but on his ability to execute and innovate around an established concept.

Entrepreneurship is more about acting on ideas, refining existing solutions, responding to market needs, and not necessarily having a new or groundbreaking idea.

Recognising the Entrepreneur Within

In this part, we provide a self-test to help you determine your entrepreneurial potential. Understanding where you are, your strengths, and areas that need improvement before jumping into entrepreneurship is vital. This exercise will give you valuable information about your current mindset and how ready you are to embark on the entrepreneurial journey.

Self-Assessment: Evaluating Your Entrepreneurial Potential

Entrepreneurship requires a specific mindset, a combination of traits, lifestyle, and business. The first step is to evaluate whether you possess or are willing to acquire these traits. The below self-questionnaire will help you reflect on your entrepreneurial readiness. It's essential to be honest with yourself because, in this way, you will have a better perspective on where you stand on your entrepreneurial path.

Self-Assessment Questions:

Resilience:

What is your response to failure?

A) I give up and feel defeated.

B) I try again but have difficulty overcoming my failures.

C) I learn from failure, adapt, and try again with an improved approach.

Creativity:

When given a problem, how do you come up with a solution?

A) I rely on old methods and ideas that will work.

B) I adhere to tried and true solutions but am open to new thoughts if necessary.

C) I believe in thinking outside the box and searching for new, innovative solutions to the problem.

Risk-Taking:

How do you feel about risk-taking?

A) I avoid taking risks whenever possible.

B) I'll take small risks, but not anything that I find too uncertain.

C) I'm at ease with planned risks and find them necessary for expansion.

Adaptability:

When plans suddenly change, what do you do?

A) I get frustrated and find it hard to adjust.

B) I try to adjust, but it is an effort and it takes some time to accept changes.

C) I quickly change, look for new options, and alter my style accordingly.

What are your strengths and weaknesses?

Think about places in your life where you are strong and places where you are weak. How do they align with the traits we have talked about? For example, if you struggle with being flexible, consider how you might become more capable of embracing change.

How do you handle uncertainty?

Think about your tolerance strategy. Entrepreneurship is a voyage into the unknown, so coping in uncertain conditions is key to achievement. Do you tolerate ambiguity, or do you find yourself seeking stability and certainties?

Developing Entrepreneurial Qualities

In the previous section, you assessed your entrepreneurial potential and reflected on successful entrepreneurs' traits. Now, let's practice developing these traits. Entrepreneurship is a skill set that can be acquired over time, and each of the four main characteristics—resilience, creativity, adaptability, and risk-taking—can be developed through intentional action and practice.

How to Build Resilience:

- Accept Failure: Understand that failure is not an indicator of your ability; it's an opportunity to learn and grow. Take setbacks as constructive lessons.

- Practice Self-Kindness: Don't be too self-critical when things are unexpected. Be gentle and understanding towards yourself when difficulties arise.

- Maintain Focus on the Greater Good: In the event of failure, remind yourself why you're working towards something big. A vision for the longer term will propel you to go on.

- Practice Perseverance: Persist even when your progress is not immediate. Break large tasks into smaller, workable steps to remain motivated.

Exercise:

Describe an experience where you experienced failure. Think about what you learned and how to use those lessons to drive your entrepreneurial career.

How to Encourage Creativity:

- Do Creative Exercises: Experiment with brainstorming sessions where no idea is taboo. Let yourself think freely and unjudgmentally.
- Look for Inspiration: Read books, go to workshops, or speak with individuals from other businesses to gain different viewpoints.
- Question Assumptions: When encountering a problem, ask yourself, "What assumptions am I making? What if there's another way?"

- Experiment with New Ideas: Pilot small ideas before making significant commitments. Use the feedback to refine and improve your method.

Exercise:

Consider a present challenge you're dealing with. Jot down at least three innovative solutions you haven't considered yet.

How to Develop Adaptability:

- Accept Change: See change as a possibility instead of a threat. The more you accept change, the less complicated it will be to adapt.
- Stay Open-Minded: Remain open to making changes and modifying your strategy depending on fresh inputs or feedback.
- Keep Learning: Flexible entrepreneurs continually learn. Inform yourself of market trends and the latest technologies.
- Diversify Your Skills: Enhance your skills to cope with various challenges. The more adaptable you are, the more flexible you will become.

Exercise:

Describe a recent experience in which you needed to think on your feet. What did you learn from that experience? How can you apply this experience to future change?

How to Develop Savvy Risk-Taking

- Weigh Risk vs. Reward: Before taking a risk, weigh the potential rewards against the risks. Ensure the potential rewards are worth the risks.
- Begin Small: Start small and build confidence in taking increasing risks as you gain more experience.
- Reduce Risks: Search for opportunities to minimise risk, including by planning, insurance, or consulting mentors.
- Learn from Mistakes: If a risk doesn't pay off, figure out what went wrong and apply the experience to make smarter decisions in the future.

Exercise:

Reflect on a risk you have taken in the past. How did you evaluate it, and what happened as a result? What would you do differently the next time?

Summarising the Key Points of the Chapter

In this chapter, we have established the groundwork for comprehending what it means to be an entrepreneur. We've discussed essential concepts crucial for anyone contemplating the entrepreneurial path, from the definition of entrepreneurship to recognising the characteristics necessary for success.

Now that we've laid the groundwork for entrepreneurship and identified the traits contributing to success, we're ready to explore the entrepreneurial mindset further.

In the next chapter, Chapter 2: The Entrepreneurial Mindset, we'll explore how to develop the mindset that will drive your entrepreneurial success.

You will discover how to shift from a traditional employee mindset to an opportunity-seeking, risk-taking, uncertainty-tolerant growth mindset.

Along this journey, you will discover how to build the mindset needed to start a business and grow and sustain it in the long run. That will include studying how to innovate, adopt strategic risk-taking behaviour, and accommodate change.

Chapter 2: The Entrepreneurial Mindset

This Chapter is your guide to developing an entrepreneurial mindset, the way of thinking that helps you succeed in business. As you shift from being an employee to becoming your boss, you'll need to think differently, act boldly and build the habits that drive a successful entrepreneur.

Being an entrepreneur isn't just about owning a business; it's about creating value and leading your life purposefully. It's about spotting chances, making bold choices and growing from every challenge. The way you think and act will shape your business and your journey..

A growth mindset will help you to stay open to improvement.—whether you select your business model, manage your team, or adapt to market change. A growth mindset will guide how you solve your problems and bounce back from failure.

In this chapter, you will learn:

- To take responsibility for your business outcomes and habits.
- Acquire the entrepreneurial attributes of resilience, flexibility, and creativity.
- Acquire the mental transposition capacity in a manner that will also augment your entrepreneurship.

Getting Inside the Entrepreneur's Mind

Employee-to-entrepreneur means stepping out of one's comfort zone and regular job—it's an ontological shift in one's mental and action responses to work, decisions, and improvement. It is a fundamental inner transformation from systematic to masterful creation, self-directed decision-making, and entrepreneurial outcomes.

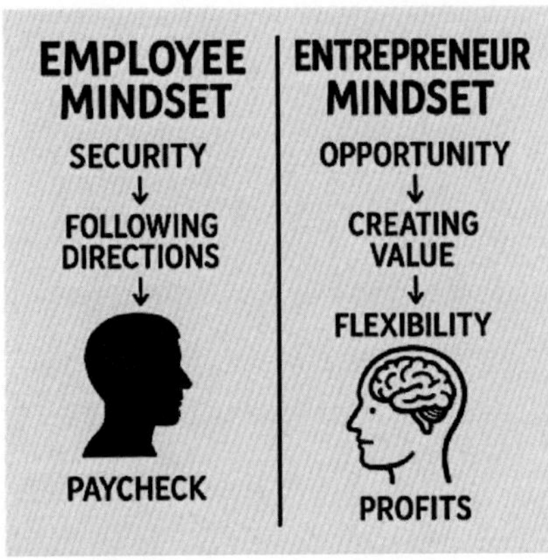

The Employee Mindset vs. The Entrepreneurial Mind

Employee Attitude: As an employee, your mind is set on doing what you are told to do, being allocated work, and having goals set by others. You are living in a shutdown plan with boundaries already established. Your choice is a spin-off of procedures already underway, and there is the buffer of your employer.

Entrepreneurial Mindset:

Entrepreneurship won't be handed to you on a silver platter; instead, you'll create it for yourself and push your business to where you need it. You must take smart risks and explore untamed lands. There never really is quite an actual "safety net," so you're the one who gets to be the one to set the goals, make it happen, and call your business where it's headed. Entrepreneurs always look to improve, innovate, and take personal responsibility for their success and business failure.

The Attitude Shift:

Shifting from employee to entrepreneur means changing how you think and act. You become a leader, the decision maker and one who takes the responsibility.. As an employee, one sees work getting done somehow, one delegates tasks to others to handle and decides for oneself. As an entrepreneur, one is left with the following:

- Leadership innovation: Continuously focus on achieving something new or creating new products/services.
- Make independent decisions: Be prepared for risk and reward, and make the decisions that will drive the business forward.

The best part is understanding that entrepreneurship is having your own business, idea, and product. It's becoming the person responsible for your success, setting your objectives, and deciding how to be successful in a world full of possibilities and uncertainty.

Curiosity, Resilience, and Flexibility

To thrive as an entrepreneur, you need three powerful traits: curiosity to explore, resilience to bounce back, and flexibility to adopt. These qualities help entrepreneurs face issues with an open mind, master something new daily, and gear up to respond to shifting realities. These qualities are helpful when navigating the entrepreneur rollercoaster and building a sustainable business.

1. Curiosity: The Motivational Force Behind Lasting Innovation and Learning

Curiosity sparks behind innovation:- Curiosity drives the urge to learn, pose questions, and do things differently. Curiosity to entrepreneurs is not learning but inquiry "why" and "how" that leads to new ideas, improved solutions, and new learning. Curiosity drives entrepreneurs to action, doing, thinking in advance, being proactive in advance of time, discovering unserved customer needs, and improving products or services.

Why It Matters:

Curious entrepreneurs stay alert. They are always learning and finding ways to stand out from the crowd. This helps them stay ahead of competitors and discover fresh opportunities that others miss.

How It Empowers Entrepreneurship:

Entrepreneurship translates curiosity into a business of innovation, learning new solutions to challenges and revealing new possibilities. Entrepreneurship makes the entrepreneur open, resilient, and committed to constant improvement.

2. Resilience: Ability to Bounce Back from Disaster

Resilience is what keeps entrepreneurs going when things get tough. Failure, rejection, or setbacks are part of the journey. What matters is how quickly you get back up, learn, and try again.

Why It Matters:

Entrepreneurship allows individuals to be focused on long-term goals even when short-term achievement is disheartening. Resilience makes them focused when others will give up and compels them to push forward with enthusiasm.

Real-Life Example:

Jack Ma is a global symbol of business perseverance. Before Alibaba, he was rejected for employment (even by KFC), rejected by over 30 companies, and failed the Chinese university entrance exam twice. Even after Alibaba's establishment, he was mocked and belittled. His original idea of an e-commerce website in China was questioned by investors and the public.

Alibaba was not profitable when it began. At one point, the company was close to bankruptcy, but Jack never quit. He had faith in the Internet, in small businesses, and in China as an emerging power in online commerce around the world. His determination allowed him to make mistakes early on, stay focused on his vision, weather criticism, cash flow issues, and competitive stress.

Today, Alibaba is a global e-commerce giant, and Jack Ma is not remembered for what he has done, but for the incalculable number of times he got back up after being knocked down.

How It Enables Entrepreneurship:

Failure is a part of the process. Resilient entrepreneurs treat failure as a lesson, not as a dead end. They grow stronger with every challenge they face.

3. Flexibility: Achievement in an Ever-Changing Business World

Business constantly changes, and the owner must learn to be flexible. Flexible entrepreneurs change their strategies, products, and business models to fit changing markets, technology, or customer requirements. This gives business professionals greater autonomy to deal with uncertainty and respond to new opportunities.

Why It Matters:

Acumen in business keeps businesspeople current and in sync with the changing nature of the market. Less adaptable players will be left behind, yet flexible business players know how to put it in gear when called upon and keep driving their business forward.

How It Facilitates Entrepreneurship:

Flexibility allows entrepreneurs to adjust whenever necessary, feel the pulse of new possibilities, and stay in the competition as situations change. Flexible entrepreneurs can adapt their strategy according to customers' needs, respond to changes in the business, and find new areas for business growth.

Risk and Uncertainty

Entrepreneurship is being in a situation with a risk, but savvy entrepreneurs don't take risks; they control them. It is natural for humans to embrace risk and uncertainty as entrepreneurs. Entrepreneurs must be able to make possible risk assumptions, be alert, and create possibilities of uncertainty. This section will deal with embracing risk and uncertainty, controlling them strategically, and coping with the fear of failure.

1. Embracing Risk and Uncertainty as the Normal State of Entrepreneurship

Uncertainty and risk are the world of the entrepreneur. Entrepreneurs must act on incomplete information and uncertain outcomes, whether launching a new product, entering a new market, or investing. Uncertainty is the mark of growth—promising entrepreneurs learn how to embrace risk, use it as a learning mechanism, and take steps to reduce its impact.

Why It Matters:

Never fear risk; face it. Risk-taking entrepreneurs will take risks, explore new frontiers, and begin their ventures. The trick is to combine planning and strategy with risk-taking.

How It Supports Entrepreneurship:

Entrepreneurs can innovate, venture into new businesses, and re-open markets through risk-taking. Innovative Risk-taking entrepreneurs with the capability to strategise and aggressive risk management are destined to excel in competitive markets.

2. Smart Risk taking -Plan before you leap

Entrepreneurs don't take wild chances; they calculate risks. They gather facts, test small ideas first, and have a backup plan ready. Smart planning turns big dreams into real opportunities.

How to Take Calculated Risks:

- Data Analysis and Research: Study the market, facts, competitors and customers.
- Begin Small and Expand: Test ideas at trim levels before sinking all resources.
- Build Safety Net: Incorporate backup plans to ensure possible failure has the least possible consequences.
- Get Advice: Discuss ideas with mentors, Partners, and successful industry professionals to develop strategies for coping with risks upon experiencing them.

3. Turning Fear of Failure into Fuel:-

The biggest challenge for an entrepreneur to be successful is the fear of failure. Fear of failure paralyses entrepreneurs and prevents them from doing anything. But failure is unavoidable in entrepreneurship; the trick is to make it a learning opportunity to enhance.

Why It Matters:

Risk-taking entrepreneurs risk missing out on enormous opportunities. Failure should be viewed as a learning experience and a stepping stone to ultimate success. Most successful entrepreneurs fail many times before they finally succeed, and they use failures as learning tools and building blocks.

Self-Discipline and Time Management Importance

1. The Importance of Self-Discipline and Time Management in Entrepreneurship

Time management and discipline are the superpowers of entrepreneurs. As an entrepreneur, you are the primary driving force of your business, and your success, to a great extent, depends on whether you can discipline yourself in whatever you do and manage time. This is particularly required when there is work, side projects, and other activities simultaneously, all of which demand your attention and focus.

Why Self-Discipline Matters So Much:

Entrepreneurship might be a situation where no organised environment is shared with a regular job, and one is liable to get easily diverted or go off course. Without self-discipline, procrastination sets in, and one cannot get things done and thrive. Self-discipline keeps entrepreneurs focused and regulates distraction and determination even when lacking motivation.

Why Time Management Matters:

You have a company, and there is only so much you need to accomplish—your company, product creativity, marketing or even customer service. Time management matters in attempting to maximise the use of precious assets such as deadline meetings, arriving on time, and utilising the time as best possible to avoid burnout. The entrepreneur is "wearing multiple hats," and knowing how to divide time among these various duties in a way that will result in long-term success is also essential.

2. Organisation, priority, and time management rules of thumb

Time-Blocking Exercise: Block time for some of your tasks or work in your day. This lets you focus on a single task and avoid diversion. Reserve some hours for client meetings, product design, and private time.

- Prioritise: Begin your day, lay out your work, and prioritise it from the most important and most urgent to the least. Prioritise the high-priority tasks most relevant to becoming successful in your business and the future. Utilise the Eisenhower Matrix as a helpful tool to sort tasks into four quadrants (urgent, necessary, neither, etc.) so you will know what to do first.
- Delegate Work: Realise that you cannot do everything yourself. Some individuals can delegate work and allow you to oversee important decisions and strategy development.
- Set up work-life Boundaries: Establish clear boundaries between work and personal life. Create time for leisure, exercise, and individual appointments. Avoid the urge to work around the clock, as burnout can quickly destroy your efficiency.
- Utilise Digital Tools: PC software such as project management software (e.g., Trello, Asana, or Monday.com)

and time management software (e.g., Toggl or RescueTime) will organise and keep you on track with your goal.

A reason for concern is that the focus is on how business is impacted through self-regulation and time management. With its tips on how to stay well-equipped, work-oriented, and accomplish excellent time management, it equips readers with all they need to remain productive and balance life against work. The expectation is to help business owners become goal-driven and burnout-resistant so they can stay efficient and productive as they grow their businesses.

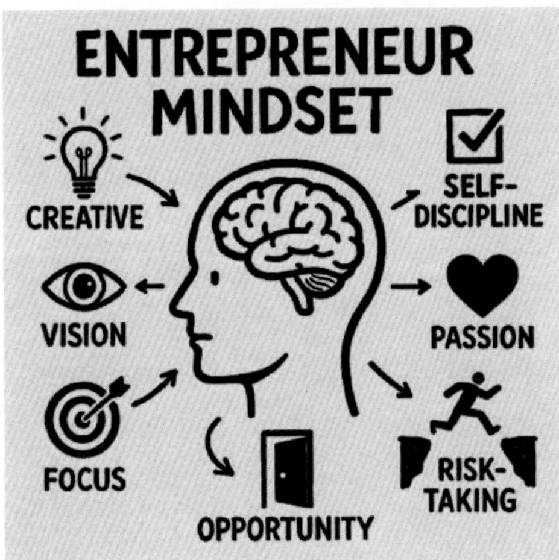

Determining Your "Why" and Being Specific When Goals Are Involved

1. Why having a clear "Why" or motivation to be an entrepreneur is vital

Your why is the heartbeat of your business. Why you do what you do is essential because it will keep all of your decisions in motion, from how you choose your goals to how you set the values and culture of your business. Your why will be the keystone of your business, psyching you up and keeping you back on track even when things aren't so sweet.

Why It Matters:

When you know your "why," you're more emotionally committed to what you're doing. Entrepreneurs have a sense of purpose, and that's the motivation to keep going when you screw up, and it inspire other people—customers, your team, and partners to believe in your journey. Example:

Simon Sinek's Golden Circle philosophy shows why the most prominent companies start with "why." Apple, for example, started with an internal purpose: to disrupt and empower through innovation. From design to marketing, it's an extension of that.

2. Clear, Measurable Goals

After you've discovered your "why," you can begin to establish definite, tangible objectives that will make your vision a reality. Goals give direction to success and enable you to track it; without goals, it's easy to get lost in the daily hustle.

Why Goal-Setting:

Goal-setting connects your vision to the real world. Goal-setting gives you a direction to work towards and reminds you of the bigger picture. Entrepreneurial goals Entrepreneurship makes entrepreneurs self-motivated, specific-oriented, and goal-directed to accomplish their goals.

SMART goals: Goal-setting through a systematic goal-setting process, i.e., SMART approach:

- Specific: Write down (e.g., "Increase website traffic by 20%").
- Measurable: Use a measurer on black, writeable paper to ensure you have a way of measuring progress toward quantitative goals (e.g., "Boost sales by 15% next quarter").
- Achievable: Choose doable objectives based on your existing ability and resources.
- Relevant: Ensure your objectives will support your mission and overall business strategy.
- Time-bound: Set a timeframe for the meeting (e.g., "Get new launch production").

3. Utilising Your "Why" as a Decision-Making Guide

Your "why" is a yardstick for making choices so that your business practice will never stray from your values and purpose. If the quality is the core of your purpose,

How to find and turn problems into business opportunities:

Great entrepreneurs don't just build products. They solve problems, complain, and spot gaps in the market, which are hidden business opportunities. They train their minds to spot these problems and turn them into products, services, or businesses that people actually need.

1. Discovery of Market Spaces and Customer Complaints
Great business folks always look around the world for something to fix. These problems arise as customer gripes, ineffectiveness within current systems, or market opportunities. Great business folks with a vision even think of such problems and invent a solution to turn difficulties into cashmakers.

- Observe the Market: For competition, watch for profitability, customer dissatisfaction, and market trends. Are customers not satisfied with what's out there? Observe for potential inefficiency or dissatisfaction.
- Ask Questions: Begin with basic questions such as: "What are most people complaining about? What type of people complain about current products or services?" These can be signs of areas to fill.
- Customer Interviews: Face-to-face customer interviews are enlightening. Interview your ideal customers and discover what is difficult for them, what they want to improve, or what might make their lives easier.

2. How Successful Entrepreneurs Find Problems and Make Solutions

Successful entrepreneurs everywhere don't just notice a problem, but rather consider how they'll fix it ahead of time, typically by envisioning new answers in the form of new businesses, goods, or services. They chart across customer needs and constraints of existing solutions to discover new solutions for existing ones.

How It Contributes to Entrepreneurship:

Entrepreneurial DNA is problem-solving and innovation when it relates to discovering new solutions. Developing a new product, developing a new current service, or determining a business model to fix an already present problem, that genius opportunity finder kind of entrepreneur can inject much value into the marketplace.

Developing an Action Plan and Vision Board:

Every incredible journey starts with a clear destination. As an entrepreneur, you need a vision for where you are heading and a plan to get there. Think of your business dream like a map. Your vision board shows your destination and your action plan.

1. The Power of a Vision Board

A vision board is a tangible reminder of your vision and dreams. It reminds you each time what you wish to accomplish in life and career. By putting images, quotes, and goals on a board, you have a potent visual reminder that reminds you of your goal and gets you into action each time.

How to Create a Vision Board:

- Step 1: Dream Big and Know Your Goal: Determine your long-term objectives. What do you want to achieve in your small business undertaking? The objectives may be business success, individual success, or success in life.

- Step 2: Find Pictures or Quotes: Identify words, images, or quotes symbolising your objectives. For example, find photos of successful start-ups or inspirational quotes if you want to begin a successful start-up business.
- 3: Build and Display: Pin your quotes and pictures onto a board or virtually in a place where you view them daily. Set your vision board where you notice it daily, like your bedroom or office.

Why It's Important:

A vision board also holds you accountable, repeatedly reminds you that you're set on the objectives, and acts as a motive to allow you to monitor progress in the long term because visions change over time.

2. Having a Credible Plan- Turn vision into action

Having a vision is only the first step. Next, you must take that turn in that vision action plan. An action plan breaks down the term vision and incremental steps. Breaking this reduces the overwhelmingness of offering goals that aren't and makes progress measurement.

How to Make an Actionable Plan

- Step 1: Create SMART Goals: Start by creating SMART goals. For instance, if your mission is product launching, your SMART goal would be to "Develop the product prototype and conduct market testing within six months."
- Step 2: Break Monumental Goals: Break your monumental goals into infinitesimal, bite-sized steps. For example, if your goal is to open up new markets for your business, break it into action steps like researching new markets, looking for potential business partners, or creating marketing campaigns.
- Step 3: Deadlines and Timelines: Make a timeline of all that needs to be accomplished, and set deadlines so you remain on schedule. This will keep you vigilant about fulfilling your desires within the time frame.
- Step 4: Establish Accountability Mechanisms: Keep yourself accountable by checking your progress periodically. Communicate your goal to a mentor, coach, or the reporting person so they can provide you with feedback and encouragement.

Why It Matters:

An action plan provides the exact guidance you need to adopt and never give up. It helps you avoid getting lost in dividing larger, scary goals into unnecessary steps. An action plan also guides you on the right path for your actions to reach a destination.

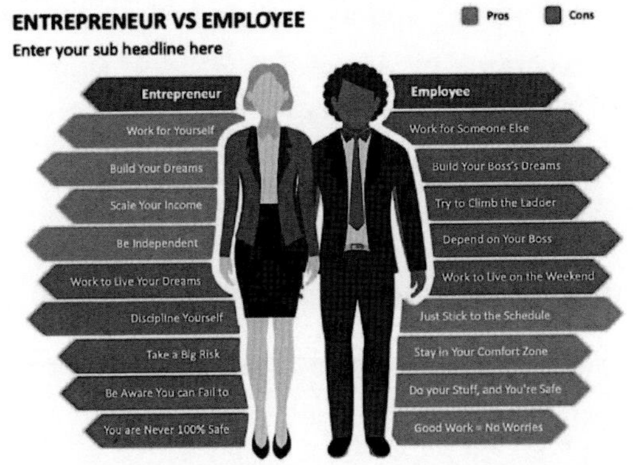

Chapter 3: Leveraging Your Employee Superpowers

How to Use Your Current Job as a Springboard: Your Job Isn't a Cage—It's a Classroom

There's a legend going around among startups: that actually to start, you're going to have to leave your job, burn your bridges behind you, and plunge headlong into the unknown. But the reality most people are too scared to say—is that your job is not your enemy. It can be your biggest platform.

Even before you begin business, your workplace is a haven where you can try out business methods, know the client psychology, and make blunders without suffering any personal financial loss. You are exposed to systems, structures, client comment loops, and conflict resolution loops in real time—all of them being the same issues that will confront you once you run a business yourself. Why not take it?

Every meeting, report, disagreement, or client interview is a real-time simulation of what will happen to one's life as an entrepreneur. By simultaneously being a participant and observer, you may discover some incredibly valuable things that many potential entrepreneurs must find the hard way—and dearly.

This chapter isn't here to tell you to quit your job. Instead, it's here to help you see your job differently. Not as a stop sign or exit door—but as a launchpad. A smoother road to the same destination.

What You Can Learn on the Job That Books Won't Teach You:-

You don't need a highly qualified degree, like an MBA, to learn how to be an entrepreneur.

You just need to start paying attention to what your daily job is already teaching you.

From your workstation, calls, and deadlines, you're learning real-world business skills, one task at a time.

- Business Strategy & Problem Solving: Working on projects or observing decision-making exposes one to long-range planning, budgeting, and market positioning.
- People Management: Intern management, conducting small projects, or observing team dynamics, learns motivation, conflict resolution, delegation, and the art of creating high-performing teams.
- Customer Handling & Selling Skills: As a customer-facing professional or support function, you're learning communications skills, overcoming objections, and empathy—all of which are necessary to understand what your future customers need.
- Leadership When Under Pressure: Working under high-pressure conditions—a product launch, a deadline looming, or a corporate crisis—prepares you to be stern and calm. You'll learn how to adapt and prioritise.

- Resource Optimisation: When you're asked to hit goals with fewer resources, you are not just working smart, you are learning to be lean and efficient.

  That mindset is gold when starting your venture with limited funds.

Everything mentioned above applies immediately to entrepreneurship. The lone exception? Work consequences are shared. As an entrepreneur, the wins and losses are all yours.

Real People, Real Proof – Micro Case Studies

Let's talk about people who turned their everyday jobs into something bigger. They didn't wait for perfect conditions or million-dollar ideas. They simply used what they already had, skills, insights, and guts to start something new.

Now, here is this in action with some micro case studies:

Sneha, working as a Customer Support Manager to a SaaS Founder: Customers complained the most about onboarding uncertainty as a foundation at a B2B SaaS organisation. From the pain points, she proposed changes in-house (that were rejected) and ultimately built an onboarding tool herself. One year later, she had paying customers and a technical co-founder, thanks to being the first training ground in the office.

Raj, D2C Brand Owner, was great at sales—he knew how to get people to say "yes." But he didn't stop there. He took what he learned on the job and used it to build a skincare brand from scratch. He wrote the product descriptions, tested them, and built a loyal customer base.

These weren't overnight success stories. These people used their jobs as training grounds, watching, learning, testing, and growing.

Their day jobs gave them a mirror to see who they were, a mentor to shape their skills, and a map to find the next step.

Finding Skills You Can Use in Business

The Power of Self-Discovery – What Are You Already Good At?

You must look inside. What do you already have to bring?

Take a quiet moment, grab a notebook or open your phone, and ask yourself ;

- What do I do so naturally that others find difficult?
- What are managers or colleagues consistently praising me for?
- When do I feel most confident at work??
- When do I think I am most self-assured or "in flow" in my career?

Answers will release patterns of hidden strengths, many of which are entrepreneurial gold.

You may be a genius at breaking down hard-to-grasp information critical to content creation, teaching, or counselling. Maybe you're the glue in your team—the one who keeps everyone connected. That's your superpower. . Don't underestimate your tendencies—most of them are your best business assets.

Core Transferable Skills and How They Show Up in Work and Business

And here we'll touch on some powerful l, high-impact skills and where they appear in business and work:

- Communication: Clear, concise communication establishes credibility and trust, whether in emails, pitches, or customer conversations.
- Negotiation: This skill helps negotiate salaries/vendor contracts, acquire clients, and secure capital.
- Financial Literacy: Balancing a team budget or checking project expenses on the job translates to business cost control, pricing strategy, and margins.
- Problem-Solving: Fixing Team issues or solving daily hurdles. That same sharp thinking helps you navigate startup chaos. Time Management: Meeting tight deadlines and juggling multiple tasks at once will help you get used to the frenetic pace of an early-stage entrepreneur.

Example: Once required to manage the minutiae of her 9–5 life, Priya established a thriving boutique event-planning business. Her proficiency in managing logistics, staff, and last-minute catastrophes after the business day disadvantaged her as a businesswoman.

Skill Mapping Framework – Know Your Tools

To help you visualise your strengths, here's a simple Skill Transfer Map you can create:

Current Role Task	Skill Used
Leading weekly team meetings	Leadership, planning
Creating performance reports	Analytical thinking, data literacy
Writing client emails	Communication, tone control

Business Relevance	Example of Application
Managing employees or freelancers	Running a remote team
Measuring business performance	Tracking ROI and KPIS

Customer engagement	Crafting sales and retention emails

Activity - here's a quick challenge for you:

1. Write down five tasks you do regularly at work.
2. For each one, ask yourself: *"How could this help me run a business?"*

   Example:

- I plan weekly schedules → That's time management.
- I calm angry customers → That's customer service and emotional intelligence.
- I make presentations → That's pitching and persuasion.

This isn't just about reflection—it's about recognising your readiness.

Case Studies of Employees Who Became Entrepreneurs

Why Case Studies Matter & Patterns of Success

We love stories, particularly the ones in which we can place ourselves in the frame. Case histories are mirrors, reflecting other individuals' paths and what is available to us. Whether a school teacher who ventured to create an ed-tech startup or a corporate analyst who founded a creative agency, actual stories spark faith and desire.
In hundreds of start-up stories, some patterns repeat:

- Stepping out on faith to start small and stay on the payroll.
- Painful realisation or moment of insight that led to action.
- Learnability to learn new skills outside the job spec.
- Using networks and in-house talent to pilot and prove ideas.
- Repetitive self-belief in the unknown.

The following case studies aren't only inspiring, but also blueprints. They show how average employees became great founders, usually by working behind the scenes until the moment was right.

Case Studies

Case Study 1: From IT Analyst to AI Start-Up Founder – Aakash Malhotra

As a seven-year-old IT analyst at a Fortune 500 firm, Aakash became increasingly frustrated with how glacially current systems embraced AI-based automation. After a company-sponsored hackathon, he became interested in predictive analytics and earned several online AI certifications on weekends and nights.

Turning Point: Having blown his workflow automation program, which his team had discovered him testing on, he understood corporate culture was not, but the market was.

Today, Aakash is an entrepreneur and founder of PredictWise, an artificial intelligence-based workflow automation platform specialising in mid-size companies. In his mind, his analytical thinking, customer interaction, and exposure to corporations propel his firm's credibility, especially when it first begins.

Case Study 2: From HR Executive to Remote Culture Consultant – Sanjana Pillai

Sanjana was an HR executive when the pandemic struck. As her organisation went virtual, she noticed a widening gap in communication, morale, and performance. She chose to spearhead internal change in remote onboarding and virtual culture building.
Turning Point: A smaller startup contacted her on LinkedIn after she published about remote team culture on LinkedIn and asked her to come in as a consultant. One led to five projects.

Today, Sanjana currently has and operates her consultancy practice, CultureCraft, where she assists remote-first startups with building compelling cultures. All those years of people managing, writing internal policies, and troubleshooting conflicts were excellent training.

Case Study 3: From Content Writer to D2C Brand Owner – Arvind Shah

Arvind worked at a content agency, penning copy for many consumer brands. He was incredibly fascinated by brand voice strategy and consumer psychology.
Turnaround Point: His one campaign flew, but the company reaped all the benefits. Fatigued but inspired, he launched his D2C brand with a storytelling push.

Present: Arvind's Zafran Tales, an organic tea business, is famous for its poetic packaging and robust Instagram presence. He still writes all the copy and initiates other copywriters into a founder mentality.

Building Skills, Networks, and Resources in Your Career Upskilling in Your Career:-

You don't need a fancy degree, a six-month break, or a massive loan to begin your business journey.

You can start learning and growing right where you are at your current job.All it takes is curiosity, commitment, and the willingness to take small, steady steps.

This is the way to upskill wisely:

- Online Certifications: We have online platforms like Coursera, LinkedIn Learning, and Udemy where we can learn business development, design thinking, coding, or digital marketing at our convenience.

- Internal Training: We must use company-provided workshops, mentorship, or learning portals. Even a leadership or communication soft skills workshop can be very beneficial.
- Cross-functional Exposure: Offer to work on cross-department projects. Working in the finance, tech, or legal departments will expose you to an understanding of how a business functions as an organisation.
- Side Projects as Your Work: Provide pilot projects or ideas from within. They keep your entrepreneurial abilities sharp, and you gain a reputation for being a problem-solver.

Smart Networking

Success isn't just about what you know.

It's also about who you know and how well they know what you can do it.

This is how you build a strong network if you are already employed:

- Be Active LinkedIn: Write sensibly about industry trends, ideas, and work. Credibility shines through visibility.
- Watch professional webinars, conferences, or networking events on weekends or evenings. You are surrounded by people already doing what you would love to do.

- Ask for Advice from Mentors: Find professionals one or two steps ahead of you and request advice. A genuine compliment, a thoughtful question, and a straightforward ask do more than make lavish introductions.
- Give Before You Take: Act positively in community discussions, support or refer others. You build trust when perceived as a giver, not a taker.

Resource Building

Resources are not money—they're tools,, knowledge, and systems that make things easier when you do start your business. But a lot of money is involved, and investing in your future as a founder is all about getting things squared away today.

Financial Planning:

- Open a "founder fund" savings account.
- Trim personal spending to have a more excellent runway when you eventually leave.
- Keep tabs on spending and know basic accounting—even on your side gig.

Market Research

- Late nights studying competition, customer behaviours, and market demand hotspots.

- Build mini focus groups or surveys out of your existing network.

Tool & Tech Readiness:

- Get proficient in tools like Notion, Canva, Airtable, Trello, or Mailchimp.
- Build templates, infrastructures, and redundancies that you can transfer to your company.

Having these available to you in advance is equivalent to having a soft landing when you eventually plunge.

Time Management Strategies, Setting Boundaries, Building a Routine

Balancing a career and a small business while walking the tight rope is like toe-tapping, but exceptionally well done with the right time management skills. This is how you can have a feasible plan:

Mastering Time Management:

- Prioritise Tasks: Start with Priorities: Every morning, ask yourself: *What matters today?*
  Focus on 2–3 tasks that will truly move you forward.

- Use Blocks of Time: Set dedicated time for your side hustle, maybe during lunch, early mornings, or after dinner. Even one focused hour a day adds up.

- Avoid Distractions: Avoiding distractions is a dream killer, whether you have a day job or a side hustle. Tools like Focus@Will, RescueTime, or simple tricks like the Pomodoro technique (25-minute bursts of work) can be your lifesaver.

Boundaries:

- If you don't set boundaries, your job and side hustle will swallow you whole.

  Open your calendar to your clients and co-workers so they know what to expect.
- Ensure you're preserving weekends or sometimes just evenings solely for rest and recovery. Hustle isn't 24/7—it's a balance game.
  Schedule workouts, walks, coffee breaks, or social gatherings. This isn't laziness—it's fuel for longevity. And remember, "A

burnt-out founder is no good to anyone. Not even to their own dreams."

Forming a Habit

Make a routine and not a rigid schedule. Your side business can be worked on in the morning for a few hours and afternoons for your career. A daily routine of having a schedule prevents inefficiency and stress.

Being flexible is the secret to success with a side hustle. If your primary job demands cut into one day, reschedule your side hustle work for another day, but do it as soon as possible.

Trying to work harder might seem noble, but it's not always wise.

Without a plan, juggling your job and side hustle can quickly become stress, sleepless nights, and burnout. You don't need to hustle harder. You need to hustle smarter. Here's how to stay productive and not burn out:

1. Prioritise Efficiency, Not Hard Work:

- Batch Tasks: Batch similar tasks together to optimise focus and efficiency. For example, spend an afternoon brainstorming and the next day producing content or building your product.

- Leverage Tools: Use productivity tools such as Trello for task management, Slack for messaging, or Google Calendar for scheduling. These tools automate your workflow and lighten your mental load.

2. Delegate When Possible:

Since your side business is booming, you don't necessarily have to do everything yourself. You are not a Superman, so delegating is the smartest move. Hire some work to virtual assistants or freelancers, or collaborate with others who can help you get halfway there.
Even in your primary profession, assigning some tasks to others whenever possible will free up time for your startup ventures.

3. Take Regular Breaks

Arrange for regular breaks to relax your mind. A walk, a mindfulness pause, or a short conversation with a cubicle mate can help relieve mental fatigue.

The Pomodoro technique, which involves working in focused blocks with breaks in between, is an excellent way to avoid burnout.

4. Sleep Is Non-Negotiable

Although sleeping less might at times seem like a sacrifice, sleep deprivation burnout can interfere with work performance and side hustle productivity.

Get at least 7-8 hours of sleep each night to be well-rested and alert.

5. Work Smart, Not Hard

Monitor progress weekly. Ask yourself: What's working, what isn't? Eliminate things that aren't moving you toward the goal.

Don't do it all or try too much at once. Incremental progress is the concept, not doing it all at one time.

Legal and Ethical Concerns—Not Treading on Your Employer, NDAS, and Moonlighting Policy

Building a side hustle is exciting, but ensure you're not accidentally crossing lines that could cost you your job or reputation. Think of this as building your business correctly, without burning bridges behind you.

Moonlighting Policies: Some companies don't mind if you have a side hustle. Others do.

Before you launch anything, check your contract. Look for words like "moonlighting" or "conflict of interest." If your side gig competes with your employer or affects your performance, it could cause trouble.

When in doubt, clarify with HR.

Non-Disclosure Agreements (NDAS):

If you've signed a Non-Disclosure Agreement (NDA), you have promised to keep certain information private. So don't use your company's data, strategies, or tools in your side business. Keep it clean. Keep it separate. Stealing ideas, even by accident, can lead to serious legal issues.

Work Product Ownership:

Make sure whatever work you do on your side of the business does not cross over into your line of responsibility in your day job. Whatever you produce when you are working (such as a product or piece of software) can legally become owned by your employer if you made it within work hours or through company facilities.

Always maintain physical and mental distinction between side hustle work and job work. That means having separate computers, emails, and locations for each.

Ethical Considerations:

Be honest with your employer if you believe that your side hustle conflicts with your work or if there are any possible conflicts. Honesty will usually solve any misunderstanding.

Be professional so that your side of the business does not impair your performance on your regular job. Employers value commitment and hard work, and consistency with one's word keeps one in good standing.

You can grow a side hustle while excelling at your full-time job.It's not easy, but with the right planning, boundaries, and mindset, it's absolutely possible. Stay honest. Stay focused. Stay kind. The goal isn't just to escape your job; it's to build something meaningful without compromising who you are along the way.

Chapter 4: Understanding the Power of Personal Branding

Personal branding doesn't stop with celebrities, influencers, and public figures. Before you say a word, your presence speaks. It whispers through your work, your energy, and your attitude. That's personal branding. It's not a logo or a flashy pitch; it's the feeling people carry after meeting you. It's how you make people feel, not just what you say.

Here's what personal branding is not:

Myth 1: Personal branding is just for "famous" people.
→ Reality: Your brand is your reputation. It's how you present your values, strengths, and personality to the world, whether an employee or an entrepreneur.

Myth 2: You need a massive following to build a brand

→ Reality: Influence is not about numbers—it's credibility, trust, and genuine relationships.

Myth 3: Personal branding is self-promotion.
→ Reality: Authentic branding about offering value and showing up as your authentic self.

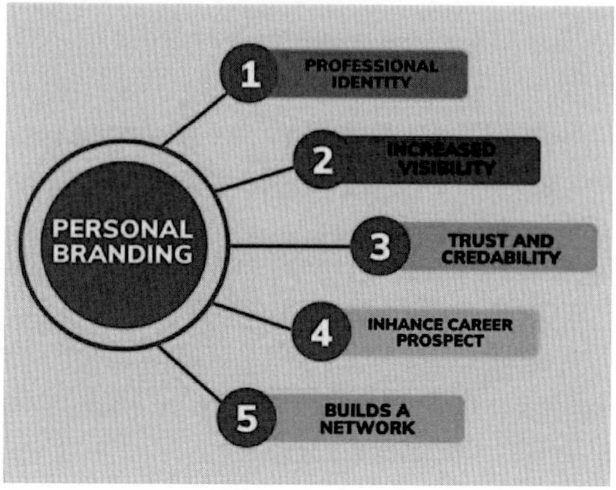

Why Personal Branding Matters?

- Can accelerate your career
- Attract mentors and give you visibility beyond your current role.
- Establish security outside your present company.
- For business owners, it
- Build confidence among investors and clients
- Open doors to partnerships
- Establish yourself as a go-to authority in your area.

Example of Personal Branding:

Shahid Khan's journey from washing dishes to owning one of the largest auto parts manufacturers in the U.S., Flex-N-Gate, is a lesson in resilience and long-term brand building. As an immigrant from Pakistan, he faced cultural, financial, and industry roadblocks early on. But instead of chasing the spotlight, Khan focused on mastering engineering precision and building trust with major automakers. Over time, his quiet persistence, strong ethics, and hands-on leadership transformed Flex-N-Gate into a billion-dollar company. Today, Shahid Khan's name is associated not just with business success but with credibility, self-made grit, and a global entrepreneurial spirit, earning him a place among America's most respected business leaders.

Crafting an Effective Personal Brand:

A strong brand isn't an accident, it's built with intention. To create a strong personal brand, pay attention to:

- **Voice**: Your tone, attitude, and energy shape how people perceive you.
- **Consistency:** Showing up regularly strengthens your presence and reliability.
- **Values:** What you believe in; your mission and passion are more than money.
- **Content Style:** The medium through which you share your know-how (video, writing, podcasting, workshops).

- **Storytelling:** Your story creates your brand. Share your wins and lessons, letting people see the real journey behind your success.

Your Digital Presence is equal to Your Silent Introduction

- Bio: Make it brief, accurate, and folks-oriented (what you do + why you do it + how you can benefit them).
- Profile Pictures: Get professional but relaxed photos on every platform.
- Personal Website: (optional but solid) - even a one-page site can be your online resume and brand headquarters.
- Social Media Profiles: Triple-check tone, images, and descriptions are the same everywhere on LinkedIn, Instagram, X (formerly Twitter), etc.

And don't forget, your online presence introduces you 24/7 even when you're not in the room.

Networking In and Out of Workplace

Internal Branding — Building Your Brand in Your Company

Your brand doesn't begin on social media—it starts in the office. Before the world knows you as a leader, your colleagues must.

Internal branding helps you build a reputation for trust, creativity, and leadership within your current company. Here's how you build it:

1. Own Projects

Offer to do new or challenging work. Leadership is not so much a name as it is doing and getting done. If you consistently get it done right, people respect you as reliable and competent.

2. Communicate with Clarity and Confidence

Be the person who simplifies complex ideas with confidence.

3. Be Visible Beyond Your Job

Participate in cross-functional meetings. Sign up for company newsletters or knowledge-sharing sessions.

Visibility isn't bragging—visibility is intentional.

4. Build Peer Alliances

Peer advocacy is the foundation of workplace branding. Assist, attribute, and celebrate success with joy—your power multiplies when individuals depend on you.

External Branding — Expanding Your Presence Beyond the Workplace

Beyond your workplace, personal branding unlocks new opportunities. While internal branding creates respect inside, e. Here's how to make a professional presence:

1. Use LinkedIn Strategically

- Optimise your profile (headline, summary, featured section)
- Share original thoughts or learnings from your work.
- Engage with leaders' posts in your field.
- Highlight achievements,

2. Start a Blog or Newsletter

If writing isn't difficult for you, start sharing your insight via Medium, Substack, or your site. Don't aim to be perfect—try to be helpful.

3. YouTube or Podcasts

If you enjoy speaking, create essential videos providing tips or answering frequent questions within your niche. Niche channels accumulate authority over time.

4. Talk to Local Colleges, Startup Events, or Webinars

You create opportunity when you get noticed and heard. Go to towns, co-working spaces, or college fests and give talks on your subject matter expertise.

On Ground Influence:

Personal branding isn't social posts—it's a matter of being where growth happens.

1. Join and Participate in Industry Meetups

Attend YourStory-organised meetups, Headstart events, Tie events, or Startup programs.

- Show up to sessions with good questions.
- Talk to speakers or fellow attendees during breaks.
- Stay connected after events via email or LinkedIn.

2. Get on Panels or Judging Boards

Most platforms welcome new voices. Join as a panellist, judge college contests, or conduct local community workshops.

3. Create a Newsletter or Forum

Post interesting industry trends every week and establish a niche audience. With 200 subscribers, your authority is established.

4. Contribute to Existing Forums

- Share your thoughts in LinkedIn groups, Reddit communities, or Quora.
- Contribute to Slack channels that are relevant to your sector.
- Post meaningful comments on relevant Twitter/X conversation.

Influence is not being famous but being valuable, reliable, and engaged.

Reaching the Right People:

Your brand isn't just your online persona—it's your reputation. And it's what makes mentors and investors listen to you, before you meet them.

1. Why Personal Branding Matters to Mentors & Investors

Mentors seek passionate, confident individuals committed to building and being good.

Investors are looking for solid, skilled entrepreneurs who can build credibility with the market. A strong personal brand—embodied by your content, communication, and consistency—demonstrates both.

2. Where to Find Mentors

- LinkedIn: Follow and connect with experienced professionals in your industry.
- Twitter/X, and Threads: Follow founders, angel investors, or VCS. Participate in the conversation, not the claps.
- Offline events: Attend panels and workshops organised by groups like Tie, Headstart, 91springboard, Y Combinator India chapters, and YourStory.
- Communities: Join carefully curated learning communities like Stoa School, The Product Folks, Leap—club, or Network Capital, where mentorship is encouraged.

3. Meeting Mentors or Investors

- Do your homework: Read about their work, philosophy, and recent activity.
- Don't ask for "mentorship" upfront: Instead, ask for their opinion on a specific problem or decision.
- Keep it brief and respectful, a strong personal brand can get the introduction over with before you shake hands. Fostering Relationships with Real Connection

Collaborate and Grow Together:-

You don't need a big platform to begin collaborating—you just need energy and open value exchange.

1. Pitching Yourself to Collaborate

Begin small:

- Approach others in your network with an audience or complementary ability.
- Suggest one idea that they can learn from and add to their audience.

2. Collaborator Types

- Instagram/LinkedIn Lives
- Collaborative newsletters or blog posts
- Guesting on YouTube, podcasts, or reels
- Product shoutouts or test partnerships

3. Being Noticed by Others

- Review or give shoutouts to your idols—most will re-post.
- Join early when creators go live (your popularity increases when others do).
- Gift something innovative and original: A sample design, a case study, or an idea that piques your interest.

4. Creating Peer Circles

- Schedule a monthly mastermind with peers of equal calibre.
- To build micro-networks, such as Airtribe, Discord servers, or WhatsApp groups.
- Bring people together—community builders will be noticed, and people will trust them.

"People do business with people. Not resumes, not titles—people they trust, respect, and remember."

Going from a Brand to a Platform

Your brand is not the destination—it's the starting point. The next step is using it as an influence platform to build communities, promote thought leadership, and be a go-to voice in your area.

1. Develop a Community, Not an Audience

- "Foster engagement beyond followers—create spaces for meaningful dialogue. Establish a newsletter, WhatsApp

group, Discord channel, or closed circle where individuals can engage with one another.
- Bring new insights, pose open-ended questions, and shine the spotlight on the members.

Example: Schbang's Harshil Karia established his sway by mentoring creators and founders and creating marketing-based content communities.

2. Thought Leadership

- Share structures, not opinions. Individuals are attracted to those who make them think better.
- Create new IPS such as "5-day startup challenge," "founder mindset journal," or "brand blueprint."
- Podcast, events, or panels, even local.
- Employ storytelling to lend your observations substance.

3. Provide Concrete Value

- Your brand becomes more legitimate when:
- You assist in gaining a customer.
- You direct someone to an asset.
- You initiate a conversation that changes minds.

"Influence isn't about popularity. It's about your ability to educate, inspire, and mobilise."

What to Avoid in Personal Branding

1. Too much self-promotion

Constantly selling yourself, your product, or your achievements turns your brand into an advertisement. Too much self-promotion kills trust. People connect more with value-centric content than with "me-centred" posts.

2. Don't Copy Others

Do not replicate somebody else's tone or pretend you know what you do not.

If you're still figuring it out, own up. Genuine journeys are sweeter than fake perfection.

3. Inconsistency Don't Disappear Randomly

Ghosting for months, posting randomly, or changing messaging too often confuses.

Pick a beat you can sustain—even one post a week can build trust over time.

4. Not listening or ignoring Feedback

Personal branding is not one-way broadcasting. It's a conversation that a great brand listens, evolves, and adapts.

Adjust your voice based on what your audience finds helpful or interesting.

In a nutshell:

Let's sum it all up:

- When you're not in the room, a personal brand is what others think about you.
- It's created by clarity, consistency, and connection.
- You don't need to scream. You just need to be yourself, be helpful, and be noticed.

Reflection Questions:

- What do I want to be known for?
- What strengths or stories make me unique?
- How do I want people to feel when they watch, see, or hear my work or content after consuming it?
- Who do I admire—and why?

Action Plan (Start Today):

- Write or update your bio (LinkedIn/Instagram).
- Pick one platform to post on regularly (LinkedIn, Instagram, Twitter/X/X, YouTube).
- Pick 2–3 pillars of content (e.g., insights from your work, book summaries, musings).
- Reach out to one inspiration or peer.

- Start a weekly post, reel, or blog—not even small, start to show up.

The most powerful personal brands aren't built overnight. They're built by showing up daily with clarity, curiosity, and conviction.

Chapter 5: Introduction to Market Research

Why Market Research Matters

Before spending your time, energy, and hard-earned money on a business idea, ask yourself this: *Do people want what I'm offering?* Market research is how you answer that question with confidence, not guesses. It gives you a flashlight in the dark, helping you find what matters, what's missing, and what people are secretly waiting for.

Market research aids you:

- To find customer pain points and likes.
- Check whether your business concept is in actual demand.
- Conduct research into competition and market niches. Based on this information, make price, product type, and brand decisions.

Whether building a technology startup, launching a fashion house, or building a coffee shop, research in the marketplace is your safety net.

Market Research

Market research is your secret weapon. Good market research doesn't just tell you *who* your customers are. It tells you *why* they buy, *what* frustrates them, and *where* you can surprise them. Market research helps you make smart moves and skip expensive mistakes.

Types of Market research:-

1. Primary Research

It involves collecting data from potential buyers, partners, or competitors firsthand, giving you fresh, up-to-date information.

Surveys: Use Google Forms, Typeform, or a face-to-face survey to accumulate likes online.

One-to-one in-depth interviews are conducted to capture the rationale and barriers.

Group discussions help to calm perception or speculation.

Observation: Observe how people utilise a product or in an environment (traffic in an area marketplace).

2. Secondary Research

This is data already gathered by another person, at no cost or for a price.

Government surveys (e.g., those carried out by the Ministry of MSMES, NITI Aayog).

Industry surveys conducted by consulting companies (McKinsey, Pwc, KPMG, etc.).

Google Trends: To know what your audience is interested in.

News articles, forums, or whitepapers: Ideal for emerging trends.

Pro tip: Combine both kinds of research. For example, you can use Google Trends (secondary) to learn about the growing demand for vegan food and a survey (primary) to determine what type of vegan products people need in your city.

Finding Your Target Market

You now know your market. You now need to figure out who your business will serve.

Demographics vs. Psychographics

Demographics (the "who"):

Age

Gender

Income level

Occupation

Education

Location

Example: Your product is a health drink. Demographics could be 25–40-year-olds from Tier 1 cities earning 8–15 lakh annually.

Psychographics (the "why"):
Values and beliefs

Hobbies and interests

Lifestyle and habits

Pain points and aspirations

Example: Psychographic characteristics could be fitness professionals interested in convenience and sustainability.

Competitor Analysis

No matter how unique your concept is, somebody else will do it.

Step 1: Identify Your Competitors

Direct competitors: Offer the identical products/services.
Indirect competitors: Meet the same customer needs differently.

Step 2: Use the SWOT Model

Create a SWOT analysis for each competitor:

Strengths
Branding, pricing, and customer loyalty
Weaknesses
Negative reviews, delayed delivery, product variety gaps, and what are their customers complaining about?
Opportunities
New trends that they have not been focusing on
Threats

Competitive funding, scalability, and other what else making them shaky.

The Role of SWOT Analysis in Strategic Decision Making

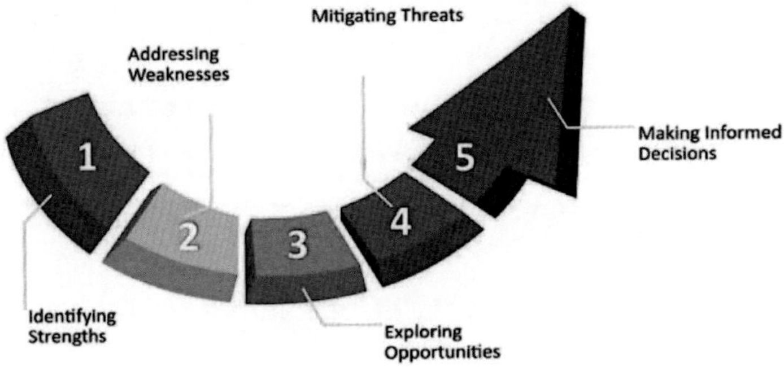

Step 3: Identify Your Opportunity Gaps

Identify spots where your competition is falling short or under-delivering.

Case Example: Paper Boat disrupted the crowded beverage category by surfing the wave of nostalgia and Indian traditional drinks with superb packaging, something significant that FMCG players had not. That space was their hook.

The Key Ingredients of a Business Plan

Executive Summary—Purpose, Main Content, How to Write It

The executive summary is the first part of your business plan that you write, but it's often the last one. It's an overview snapshot— a quick impression of your vision, business potential, and highlights.

Purpose of the Executive Summary

- Grabs attention in the first 2 minutes.
- Bashes through your business plan and value proposition.
- Demonstrates you're serious and ready.

Key Elements to Include

- Business name & idea: What are you creating and why?
- Problem you're solving: Actual pain points of your target market.
- Your solution: Brief description of your product/service and how it benefits.
- Target market: Who you're serving.
- Competitive advantage: Why you'll beat out others.
- Business model: How you'll make money.
- Financial highlights: Revenue estimate, funding request, or break-even point.
- Vision: Where do you see the business in 3–5 years?

Here's how your research becomes strategy:

- Industry overview: Growth trends, size, future potential.
- Customer persona(s): Quickly state who your ideal customers are.
- Competitor insights: Top competitors, their weaknesses, and your advantage.
- Opportunity: Why is the time now for your idea?

Marketing Strategy

Explain how you'll attract, convert, and retain customers:

- Positioning: Where your brand stands in the customer's mind.
- Channels: Social media, Google Ads, events, influencer marketing, etc.
- Pricing strategy: Cost-plus, freemium, tiered pricing, value-based pricing.
- Retention: Loyalty programs, customer service, and feedback loops.

Operational Plan

Details about how your business will run daily:

- Location: Online or physical?
- Suppliers: Who are your partners or vendors?

- Technology: Tools, platforms, apps.
- Team: Current and future hires, key responsibilities.
- Logistics: Shipping, inventory, packaging, and quality control.

Financial Projections—Cash Flow, Revenue Model, Expenses, and Break-Even Analysis

This is usually the most intimidating aspect, but let's not. Straightforward projections enable individuals to grasp how your business will scale and continue.

Revenue Model

How will you earn money?

- Direct sales (products or services)
- Subscription
- Commission or brokerage
- Advertising
- Freemium → Premium upgrades

Cash Flow Forecast

Shows your expected inflows and outgoings for 6–12 months.

Have a straightforward month-by-month format:

Month	Revenue	Expenses	Net Cash Flow
Jan	1,20,000	80,000	40,000

Feb	1,60,000	90,000	70,000

Operating Expenses

- Rent
- Salaries
- Marketing
- Raw materials
- Tech subscriptions
- Delivery & packaging

Tip: Keep a buffer of 10–15% for surprises.

Break-Even Analysis

When your revenue = cost.
When your fixed monthly expenditure is 100,000 and every unit gives you 100 profit, you'll be at break-even while selling 1,000 units.
"We will reach break-even in 8 months after launch by enrolling 300 repeat users with a monthly average spend of500."

Testing Your Idea with Minimal Resources (MVP)

What is an MVP and Why It's Important
A Minimum Viable Product (MVP) is the bare minimum iteration of your service or product that addresses the central issue for early adopters. It assists you:

- Launch faster
- Spend less
- Learn quicker
- Avoid perfection paralysis

Examples:
Zomato: It began as a basic blog called "Foodiebay" with restaurant menus in Delhi. It tested user interest before evolving into a full-fledged app.

Various MVP Forms

Landing Pages: Create a minimalist one-page website that offers your concept. And invites people to "sign up" or "show interest."

- Tools: Carrd, Webflow, Wix
- Prototypes: Figma or Canva visual mock-ups or app demos.
- Service-Based MVPS: Manually deliver the service to validate demand.
- Freemium Models: Provide a lite (free) version with limited functionality to onboard users (often for tech tooling).
- Concierge MVP: Do everything manually to learn from every customer before automating.

How to Gather Feedback, Iterate, and Pivot

Step 1: Launch it quickly—don't wait until it's perfect. Done is better than perfect.

Step 2: Interview users

- Ask them what they liked, disliked, and wish there were.
- Do short interviews or post-purchase surveys.
- Read between the lines—see what they do, not what they say.

Step 3: Measure what matters. Monitor metrics such as:

- Signups
- Repeat usage
- Drop-off points
- Purchase interest

Step 4: Iterate or pivot

- If 60 %+ users like the product → build more
- If feedback indicates a different need → pivot (reinvent)
- If nobody cares → reframe the underlying problem you're solving.

Case: UrbanClap (now Urban Company) pivoted from a listings directory to a full-service model based on user feedback around trust, quality, and availability.

Setting Short-Term and Long-Term Goals

Introduction to Goal Setting — Strategic Planning Significance
Goal setting is the key to intentional business growth. Without goals, your activities can be aimless, reactive, and less effective.

Why goal setting is significant:

- Give direction to day-to-day decision-making.
- Increases personal and team accountability.
- Enables monitoring of progress and course-correcting when necessary.
- Reminds the team of the business vision and keeps them energised.

Look at short-term objectives as stepping stones and long-term goals as your destination. Strategic planning connects where you are with where you should be.

"Failing to plan is planning to fail."
— Benjamin Franklin

How to Track Progress, What to Look Back On and Set with Vision Alignment

Setting goals is the beginning. You must have systems of monitoring and reflection for them to be effective.

1. Break up goals into milestones
Significant goals need to be subdivided into weekly/monthly checkpoints.
Example: Goal is 500 sales within 3 months → 42/week.

2. Use tools to monitor progress

- Trello, Asana, Notion: task tracking
- Google Sheets: simple tracking tables
- Habit trackers or Kanban boards

3. Schedule review sessions
Weekly check-in for short-term objectives
Monthly/Quarterly reviews for longer-term objectives

Ask:

- What's going right?
- What's getting off-track?
- Do we need to adjust the objective?

4. Stay in alignment with the vision

Review whether your goals remain consistent with your overarching mission and values.

"Are we ascending the correct peak?"

How to Pitch Your Idea to Investors or Partners

A great pitch is not a pitch; it's fire.

What makes a Great Pitch: Structure, Storytelling, Clarity, market potential, and your unique idea.

Pitching is not information—it's selling. You're selling your idea, not a product.

Needs of a good pitch:

1. Hook (1 min)

Begin with a good start—a statistic, a story, or a common problem.

2. Problem → Solution (1 minute)

Describe the problem in the real world, and then your solution.

3. Market opportunity (1 minute)

Demonstrate the potential market (size, trends, target market).

4. Product demo (2 minutes)

Describe or demonstrate your product—preferably with evidence (testimonials, prototype, video).

5. Business model (2 minutes)
How do you generate revenue? Sources of revenue and pricing.

6. Traction (1 minute)
Describe what you have already done—sales, users, partnerships, feedback.

7. Team (30 seconds)
Emphasise why your team is best positioned to win.

8. The ask (30 seconds)
Just state how much you require and for what:

Investor Expectations — Traction, Team, TAM/SAM/SOM, Financials

Traction: Paying Users, sales, retention, feedback

Team: Skill, perseverance, hustle, chemistry

TAM/SAM/SOM: overall market demand

Financials: Unit economics (CAC, LTV, margins), burn rate, break-even

Negotiating Smart, Staying Clear of Red Flags, and Building Durable Partnerships

Negotiation Strategies:

- Know your minimum acceptable terms (valuation, equity, board control).
- Avoid rushing—ask questions and negotiate offers.
- Choose investors who *add value*, not just money
- Communicate often, stay transparent

Investor Red Flags:

- Demands too much equity too soon
- Unreasonable control
- No domain expertise or network
- Overpromising "mentorship" with no accountability

Forming Strong Partnerships:

- Choose partners that share your vision.
- Communicate regularly and truthfully.
- Share updates, successes, and failures.
- Treat them as collaborators, and not cheque-signers.

Chapter 6: Financial Planning and Readiness

Starting a business without financial planning is like jumping out of a plane without a parachute—thrilling until you realise the ground is approaching fast. Most startups do not become profitable for months or even years. Without financial stability, the pressure to pay rent, bills, or put food on the table can stall decision-making and lead founders to make regrettable sacrifices or succumb to premature failure.

Why Financial Planning Matters

- Peace of Mind: A financial cushion lets you focus on growth, not survival.
- Avoidance of Debt: A financial cushion prevents reckless borrowing and **painful debt traps**
- Thoughtful Decisions: You can experiment with ideas, hone them, or wait for the ideal investor, without desperation, and make decisions.

Creating a 6–12 Month Cash Cushion

Use Runway Rule- How Long Can You Stay in the Air? Before quitting your job, calculate your **6–12 month runway**—the cash needed to cover bare essentials while your business takes off.

How to do it:

- List monthly expenses for the bare necessities, like rent, food, electricity, insurance, and EMIS.
- Multiply the figure by 6 or 12.

Understanding Personal Burn Rate

Your **burn rate** is the speed at which you spend money. Just like a rocket needs enough fuel to reach orbit, your savings need to sustain your startup, but every entrepreneur should know their burn rate, too.

- Track your fixed (non-negotiable) and variable (negotiable) expenses monthly. Use this to:
- Stretch your savings longer.
- Make realistic business timelines.
- Plan when you will need side income.

"If your burn rate is too high, your dream will burn all its fuel before it can fly."

Future Founder's Budgeting

Budgeting is not glamorous, but it is your first tool for wealth, freedom and independence. As a future founder, you must save more, reduce waste, and prepare the company.

3-Step Budgeting:

- Track: Write down every expense for at least 30 days.
- Categorise: Necessities (rent, bills), growth (learning, hardware), indulgence (dining out, shopping)
- Cut & Reinvest: Take 10–20% and cut and reinvest it into business savings.

Tools to Monitor Spending

Keep simple tools initially and build on from there. Some of the most common ones are:

- Excel or Google Sheets – free, editable, basic
- Walnut, Money Manager, or Mint – cash tracking and budgeting software
- Goodbudget or YNAB – for envelope budgeting and long-term budgeting

Pro Tip: Schedule a weekly money check on Sunday evenings; it renews priorities.

Frugal Living Tips by Indian Entrepreneurs

Some Indian founders have bootstrapped their early stage by living a frugal and Spartan life.

Ritesh Agarwal (OYO): I stayed in backpacker hotels around India to absorb and save on travel expenses.

Sridhar Vembu (Zoho): Worked out of a small town to maintain low overheads and employ cheap talent.

Peyush Bansal (Lenskart): Invested in tech and talent too early, did not splurge on office comforts.

Lesson? Don't spend on an affluent lifestyle. Spend judiciously.

Pre-Launch Investments: Save or Spend Where?

You do not have to empty your bank account to make your startup successful —you just need to spend smart.

Where to Spend:

- Training
- Domain, simple website, email ID
- Prototypes or MVP tools
- Market or test market research

Where to Save

- Workspace (coffee shops or work from home)

Rule of thumb: Spend only on that which creates clarity, feedback, or revenue-generating assets.

Short and Long Investment Ideas

Don't keep money idle —make it work for you.

Safe short-run options:

- FDs (Fixed Deposits) – liquid and safe, especially with sweep-in accounts
- Liquid Mutual Funds – higher returns than a savings account, very minimal risk

Long-term plans

- SIPs in Mutual Funds – best to build a corpus
- PPF (Public Provident Fund) – long-term savings with relief on taxation
- NPS (National Pension Scheme) – when making long-term retirement plans

Preparing for Unpredictable Income

Startup income isn't smooth—it's more like a rollercoaster. Start preparing by:

- Having a bare minimum monthly survival budget ready
- Living lean ahead of time to get used to uncertainty
- Setting up 2–3 side income streams (freelancing, consulting, etc.)

And if your pocket and head are in preparation for it, the leap doesn't appear quite so scary.

Estimating the costs of starting and running your business realistically is critical before launching. Misjudging these can derail your venture before it even begins.

One-Time Costs

These are initial expenses you'll incur just once at the time of setting up:

- Business registration and licenses
- Website development
- Branding and logo design
- Initial equipment or inventory
- Prototypes or MVP development
- Legal or consultancy fees

Recurring Expenditure

These are the regular monthly/quarterly spending that will keep your business running:

- Freelancers' wages/salaries
- Rent (if you lease offices/warehouse)
- Subscriptions (Zoom, Canva, marketing suites, CRMS)
- Marketing and advertising costs
- Hosting website, emails, and maintenance
- Travel and communication costs

Use software like Excel, Zoho Books, or QuickBooks.

Usually Underestimated Expenses

The majority of business owners neglect these in their initial budget:

- Trademark or domain renewal
- Payment gateway fees
- Trial-to-paid tool conversions
- Employee benefits or professional tax
- Software updates or technical support
- Foreseeing the need to evade future cash flow surprises by controlling small leaks.

Bootstrapping – Pros, Cons, and Real-Life Implementation

Growing your business without investors? That's **bootstrapping**—a lean, independent approach

Advantages:

- Complete decision control
- No investor influence and no ownership dilution
- Fosters lean, innovative thinking
- Builds long-term fiscal responsibility

Drawback:

- Limited or slow growth rate
- No padded budget to hire or grow
- Personnel Financial stress

When and How to Bootstrap Smartly

When to:

- You have modest startup capital needs (services, coaching, software).
- You would instead test your model first, before raising money.
- You have driven early momentum independently.

How to:

- Freelance/part-time income during business growth
- Collaboration among other founders
- Low/no-cost tools: Notion, Canna, Mailchimp, WordPress
- Investing early profits in the company

Some Bootstrapping Examples

- Wingify (Paras Chopra): Bootstrapped out of a small Delhi room —reached $10 million+ ARR.
- Kayako: Bootstrapped for more than a decade before selling.

Funding Options – The Right Way

If bootstrapping doesn't work, or you need to scale fast, you'll have to consider funding options.

Sources of Funding:

- Angel Investors- High-net-worth individuals offering capital + mentorship.
- Venture Capitalists (VCs) are Investors providing large-scale funding for equity
- Crowdfunding: Raise money from the general public through pre-orders or equity via Ketto, Wishberry, etc

Startup Loans

Low-cost or collateral-free loans under government schemes.

Credit Guarantee Scheme

Start-up loans from financial institutions.

Making the Right Choice

Ask yourself the following before fundraising:

- Do you want to grow quickly or stay small and independent?
- Are you willing to give up equity?
- Is your business socially acceptable?
- Do you need mentorship, or do you need money only?

"Raising money is not the goal. Building a sustainable business is." – Every brilliant founder

Common Financial Challenges of New Businesses:

- Inflating revenue in initial estimates
- Underestimation of costs, especially marketing or operations
- Unusual cash flow, especially service or seasonal business
- Expanding or adding personnel too quickly
- Mixing business and personal expenses

How to Create a Risk Cushion:

- Establish a 6–12 month risk cushion of minimum bare living expense + minimum bare business operation.
- Keep contingency funds for such worst-case events as loss of a major client or unexpected cost spike.
- Keep low fixed expenses in the starting phase—no long-term rent or full-time staff until unavoidable.

Lessons from Failed Startups:

- TinyOwl: Aggressive investment with no financially feasible sense.
- Stayzilla: Experiencing problems in working capital and topline, unable to grow sustainably.
- Tazzo: A Cycling rental start-up venture that failed based on unit economics and burn problems.

"Failure to plan financially is planning to fail."

Management of Debt—Good and Bad

Good Debt vs Bad Debt:

Type	Good Debt	Bad Debt
Purpose	Business expansion, skill training	Personal luxury, unplanned credit
Return	Potential ROI	No financial return
Examples	MSME loans, education loans	Credit card for shopping, payday loans

Familiar Debt Weapons:

- Credit Cards: Easy to juggle small-time cash flows, but risky.
- Personal Loans: Do not go in except under an instalment regime.
- EMIs: Never exceed 30% of the monthly salary.

Keeping a Clean Credit Rating:

- Pay EMIs and charge-card bills on time.

- Do not use all available credit.
- Check your CIBIL score now and then using apps like CRED, Paytm, or BankBazaar.

Aids:

- OneScore (for tracking credit health)
- Cred (reminder for credit card payments)
- ClearTax (repayment schedule and debt tracking)
- Cash Flow Planning for Irregular Cash Flow

Planning for Irregular Income:

- Make a worst-case income-based base budget each month.
- Save "cash cushions" received during good months for lean months.
- To begin with, place regular commitments (such as full-time workers or long-term subscription plans) on the fringes.

Pay Yourself a Salary

- However little, set aside a fixed sum each month for yourself.

Business and Personal Expenditure Segregated:

- Maintain a separate business account.
- Clean books for taxation, investor awareness, and money planning.
- Make an Emergency Revenue Plan
- Keep a list of readily salable products/services.

- Watch prices, reduce cost, or forego the use of off-season advertising.

Reading Basic Financial Statements

Intelligent decision-making depends on reading financial statements without fail.

Profit & Loss (P&L):

- Graph income, expenses, and profit over time.
- Helps with the monitoring of profitability and cost structure.

Cash Flow Statement:

- Track cash coming in and going out for your company.
- Shows liquidity, along with paper profits.

Balance Sheet:

- Gather all the assets, liabilities, and net worth into one statement.
- Provides a snapshot of business health.

"Revenues are vanity, profits are sanity, and cash is king."

Learn Key Terms:

Gross Margin, EBITDA, Runway, Burn Rate, Working Capital, Capex vs Opex

Budget Forecasting for Startups

Construct a Forecasting System:

- Utilise the available historical data to project future revenue and costs.
- In consideration of seasonality, growth strategy, and new product introductions.
- Tracking Expenses: Utilising Zoho Books, QuickBooks, or MS Excel.

Break into fixed cost, variable cost, and periodic cost.

Income Projection:

- Use a conservative stretch case and an aggressive base case.
- Calculate your break-even revenue every month.

Tip: Use rolling forecasts—recycle and refresh each quarter.

Profitability vs Growth – Trade-Offs
Growth vs Profitability:

Growth = investing (team, tech, marketing)

Profitability is the death of growth, but it builds stability.

Breakeven Analysis:

Where revenue = costs (not profit or loss).

It is profitable to know how many units you need to sell monthly to break even.

Know Unit Economics:

- Per-unit profit vs cost.
- Researches reveal scaling problems: if you lose 10 per transaction, the volume will damage you more.

Promising founders don't just build—They calculate.

Diversifying Sources of Income and Developing Good Financial Habits

One of the best money sayings is not to keep all your eggs in one basket. Even before and throughout the initial stage of your entrepreneurial journey, diversify sources of income. That may be consulting in your niche, freelancing, conducting workshops, or earning money for skills on Upwork, Clarity. Building passive income streams, like content monetisation, affiliate marketing, stock dividends, or even rental income, entails a cushion of money when money from your startup slows or comes infrequently.

Building sound money habits is no less critical. Slight but persistent habits such as daily tracking of expenses, saving and then spending discretionary income, and making on-time bill payments can prevent wasteful money leaks. Creating a habit of monthly budgets and reviewing your financial goals quarterly can work miracles in your financial decisions. Entrepreneurs who develop such habits in their formative years can ride the rollercoaster of startup life and avoid money mistakes fueled by stress.

Insurance and Tax Planning Basics

Many first-time entrepreneurs overlook one central area of financial protection: insurance. A comprehensive personal health insurance plan is non-negotiable, especially when leaving the security of a salaried job. A term life insurance policy protects your dependents financially if anything happens to you. It's also wise for business owners to consider business liability insurance, especially if they're operating in domains with legal, customer-facing, or operational risks.

Tax planning and tax compliance are equally important. Your income is rising, and so is your tax. You must know about the fundamentals of the taxation system. If you are planning to operate a business entity, seek guidance from a CA (Chartered Accountant) so that you understand your reporting requirements and minimise your tax outlay. By investing a portion of income each month, tax planning during the year lowers end-of-year pressure and encourages better financial discipline.

Recap, Financial Readiness Checklist, and Reflection

- Financial preparedness can be your most significant defence while venturing into entrepreneurship. This chapter has covered everything from emergency capital and MVP budgeting to startup expenses, investor readiness, and taxes. But facts are not power unless you do something with them. To further help you, here is a quick financial readiness checklist:
- Do you have 6–12 months of personal runway in the bank?
- Are individual and business finances separated?
- Do you know your startup's break-even and monthly burn? Did you invest when times were hard or spend on your earnings?
- Are insurance and tax returns up to date?

Be honest: "Am I financially ready to leap? What can I do in the next 30 days to move closer?"
Remember:- <u>Entrepreneurship is half innovation and half survival; most successful businesses are founded on a sound financial platform.</u>

WIN
WORK
TIME
DREAM
IDEA

Chapter 7: Scaling Heights: Growing Your Dream

Indicators You're Poised for Growth

It's thrilling to begin a business, but it becomes challenging for growth. So, the ideal time to grow is when many building blocks are in front of you. Consistent revenue is one. Suppose your business is not only breaking even but producing consistent monthly profits. In that case, it is an excellent indication that your core product or service has established a strong foundation in the market.

Second, demand exceeds your current capacity. If you are receiving repeat orders, you have strong customer retention, or you have waiting lists, that demand is crying out for a surge.

Third, **Constructive Complaints**: When customers ask for features or products you don't yet offer, they show you the path to expansion. Growth isn't driven by ego. It's powered by demand.

The Art of Strategic Expansion

When the time is right, the question is what to build next. One of the most prevalent responses is to develop more products or services, preferably complementary to your existing customer base

Upselling and cross-selling are risk-free expansions. You can sell Premium models, more lucrative products or services, or packages that increase the average ticket per buyer without necessarily getting new ones.

Second, expanding into new markets—geographic (e.g., from a city to tier-2 cities), or demographic (expanding to a new set of customers). Social media and online channels have provided more than ever, without huge capital outlays.

Case study of successful Entrepreneurs Diversifying

Consider the case of Aman Gupta's boAt, which started with mass audio products. Noticing how much people were into looks and sound, boAt started exploring wearables and lifestyle products. boAt now works with smartwatches, gaming products, and grooming products.

Building the Right Team :

Typically, operations or support are the first to be hired—admin, customer support, or social media—to give the founder space to breathe and scale. In tech startups, maybe a backend engineer; in content startups, perhaps an author or editor. The pilot virtual assistant or freelancer is occasionally hired to test the waters.

A rule of thumb is to hire to eliminate bottlenecks and reserve yourself for high-leverage tasks such as strategy, partnership, and product development.

Hiring Process Principles

The hiring process need not be sloppy but should be intentional. Begin with an excellent job description that includes tasks and what success in this position will look like.

When prospecting, utilise referral networks, such as LinkedIn and AngelList. Founders also do not sufficiently use employee and personal network referrals.

Interviewing: Don't just test technical abilities; test culture fit, adaptability, and drive. Use situational interviewing. A sample question would be, "If we were overdue on a client deadline, what would you do?" Walk them through how they'd pull it off and whether their vision aligns with yours.

Delegation - Founders' Super Power

Founders struggle with delegation because they don't wish to relinquish it, not because they distrust it. Correct this by delegating SOPs for humdrum operations. These confer quality and grant training.

Secondary is trust. Provide ownership in tasks, and don't micromanage; micromanaging is a scaling killer.

Begin small: delegate where ends, rather than means, are critical, and build responsibility.

Finally, set up weekly check-ins. Utilise them to clear priorities, get unstuck, and provide feedback. It's less micromanaging and more empowering. As your business grows, so should your leadership, growing from doer to empowerer.

Defining and holding on to your mission and core Values. As your company expands, it's easy to fall head over heels for pursuing growth figures—users, revenue, and reach. Mission creep is a quiet killer, however. A company that loses sight of why it began will lose its edge, personality, and loyal fans.

That's where you must understand and put down your core purpose—why are you here other than earning money? And your core values. Are you affordable? Do you tell the truth? Innovative? Sustainable? When you decide on a new hire, product launch, or promotion, these values must be your north stars.

Imagine your business as a tree: its branches may spread off into many different directions, but its roots—its mission and values—must be solid. Diverge or diversify as you must, but your "why" must come from your "what" and "how."

To prevent harm to this root system, build mission checks into decisions. Ask yourself: "Is this alliance, product, or growth consistent with who we are and who we're becoming?"

How to Stay on Course—Leadership Communication, Culture Building, Feedback Loops

Alignment begins at the top. Senior leadership and founders need to model and sometimes restate the mission. Founder-led team check-ins, newsletters, or town halls are great ways to align everyone, especially in remote or hybrid teams.

Culture matters. Great company culture isn't free lunches and office art; it's habits, mores, and routines. Discover excellent performance in your startup. Success is necessary, but it also promotes work that sustains your values (e.g., a customer meltdown diffused by an employee with integrity and compassion).

Give the employees the freedom to cry foul if they sense gaps between locked-up values and actual decision authority. Anonymous feedback cards, frequent one-on-ones, and retrospectives should make the firm self-aware and self-acting.

Scaling sustainably isn't about having nothing to do with a struggle, but it has everything to do with growth while remaining faithful to the essence of your startup.

Operational Efficiency Through Tools (CRM, Project Management, Automation)

As a startup expands, inefficiency compounds. What was excellent with a small team and a spreadsheet isn't excellent with more people and processes. Tools and systems come to the rescue here. Operation efficiency is not merely about speed—it's shape, reliability, and scale.

Category	**Tools**	**Why It Matters**
Project Mgmt	Trello, Asana, ClickUp	Stop drowning in sticky notes.
CRM	Zoho CRM, HubSpot	Turn leads into loyal fans.
Automation	Zapier, Mailchimp	Replace busywork with bots.

Scaling Finances—Cash Flow Management, Reinvestment Strategy

Scaling does not always mean revenue growth; it also means spending smart. Any startup is fundamentally failing at this juncture due to cash flow management. Remember that profitability on the books doesn't necessarily mean cash in the bank.

Build a solid cash flow projection model by projecting your income and expenses for the next 3–6 months.. Have a cushion for that slow month or some other unseen expense.

Don't be lured into pocketing it or spending it on a spree as profits flow. Invest in growth-initiating fundamental initiatives—tech, talent, and marketing. For example, spending money on better backend infrastructure or hiring a growth marketer will be worth it in the long run.

Second, pay close attention to unit economics, the cost of acquiring and serving a customer, and the revenues they generate. This will serve you well to scale.

Servicing Clients/Customers at Scale—Support Teams, CRM Strategies

The more customers you have, the harder it will be to deliver one-on-one, high-quality service—unless you plan carefully ahead.

Begin by creating a support foundation. Hire a customer success team or one customer success individual, an onboarding team or one onboarding individual, and an issue resolution team or resolver. Even a tiny, high-quality support team and SOPs will significantly improve satisfaction and retention.

Your CRM strategy has to go beyond data storage. Segment for follow-up, personalise messaging, and predict client needs. For instance, e-commerce businesses may use behaviour information (abandoned cart, prior purchase history) to make the correct offers. B2B businesses can use CRM notes to recall past conversations and provide pertinent solutions.

Offer several touchpoints—email, phone, WhatsApp, live chat—and track resolution time and customer sentiment through Freshdesk or Zendesk. Collect input through NPS (Net Promoter Score) or CSAT (Customer Satisfaction) surveys.

Lastly, empower your clients—spend more on knowledge bases, FAQS, or video guides that enable customers to self-fix minor issues. Not only does this improve their experience, but it also lessens some of your support staff's workload.

Avoiding Burnout—Time Blocking, Health Habits, Mental Health

Scaling a business is thrilling, but it's draining. Founders burn out from trying to manage strategy, hiring, sales, and operations simultaneously. Without intentional self-care, that hustle turns into burnout. The solution is building boundaries, establishing energy, and building sustainable habits.

Start with time blocking. Allocate specific chunks of the day to each work category: deep work (strategy, brainstorming), admin (calls, emails), and rest (meal breaks, walk breaks, non-work time). Use tools like Google Calendar or Notion to create visual blocks to remind you to remain focused and disengage when needed.

Flourish in non-negotiable health routines in your schedule. It might be a 20-minute walk or a 10-minute meditation. Your body and mind fuel your business to run—don't skimp. *You can't scale a company running on fumes.*

Building a Leadership Mindset—Trusting Your Team, As you mature, your job as a founder needs to shift from doing it all to intention-leading. That is difficult, especially if you have done it all from day one, but it is necessary so that you can build something larger than yourself.

Start with a leadership adage. Have vision, strategy, and alignment. Your role is to steer the ship, not row all the oars. This is where you make faith real—gathering people you trust, setting clear expectations for direction, and getting out of the way. There will be mistakes made, but micromanaging kills growth and morale.

Use weekly check-ins to stay connected with your team's progress without hovering. Encourage initiative, ask for feedback, and reward results, not just effort. Empower your team to solve problems, creating a culture of accountability and innovation.

Most importantly, zoom out regularly. Take a month's day or a week to stare at your purpose, review growth metrics, and brainstorm. Get lost in abstraction so you can think big, not just as an administrator but as a visionary, which your company needs.

Reflection + Planning Worksheet: Are You Scaling With Intention

Expansion is excellent, but planned expansion creates success over time. Take this final section to glance around, get a feel for where you are now, and then make your next step.

Reflection Questions:

Am I completely clear on why I want to expand now?

What structure and support do I have in place to manage increased volume?

Is the pace we are moving at right now sustainable mentally, emotionally, and financially?

Are my employees implementing our vision for the future?

What work am I still performing that I can outsource to somebody else?

Your Scalable Roadmap:

Month	Focus	Key Goal	Resources/Support Needed
1	Operations	Automate X workflow	Hire a consultant / Use [tool]

2	Hiring	Fill [role] position	Job portals / Referrals
3	Productions	Launch [new offering]	Design, testing, MVP
4	Marketing	Increase reach by 25%	Collaborations, paid ads
5	Leadership	Offload [task] completely	Train/mentor a team member
6	Wellness	Implement three wellness habits	Therapy, time off, retreats

Remember:- Scaling isn't about just going faster—it's about growing without breaking.

Chapter 8: The Entrepreneur's Clock: Mastering Time and Productivity

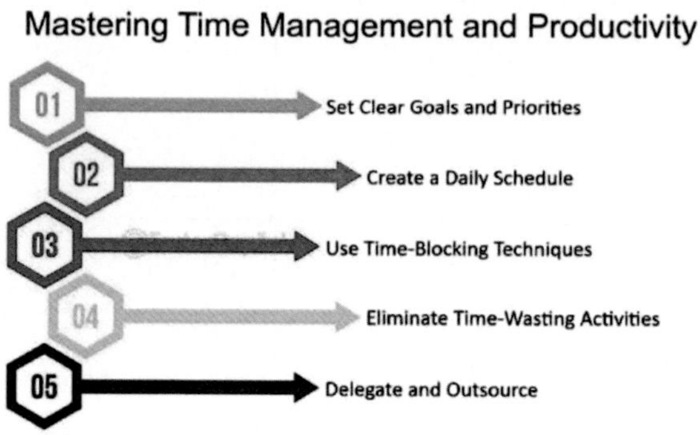

The Double-Life of a Dreamer- Balancing a Job and a Vision

A particular type of exhaustion comes from living your dream and working full-time. It's not exhausting physically—it's in your mind. This is the paradox of the modern dreamer—the employee-entrepreneur. It's not exhaustion that weighs you down; it's the endless mental shift between survival and ambition.

Let's take Neha's example. She spends Monday to Friday of every week as a graphic designer at an MNC, but at nights and on weekends, she works designing brand identities for small businesses under her name. All these years, she was merely "always busy," her friends felt. But they didn't experience the thrill of watching one of her clients roll off with her brand on the package. She was not freelancing. She was creating something for herself.

You can't keep these two worlds at the same time. You sometimes feel like you've lost your mind. It's all about time management. Time isn't money. It's your anchor. You can lose money and recover it. You can do something wrong and correct it. Time lost, however, is gone.

Setting Realistic Priorities

When everything is a priority, nothing gets done. Most side hustlers are guilty of this, adding 15 items to their to-do list daily and then getting discouraged when half of them fall through. The solution is the Must-Should-Could system.

Rather than creating a monster list, separate your daily or weekly objectives into three categories:

- Must: Priorities. Things that directly affect your job or business
- Should: Valuable but not urgent (e.g., brainstorming new ideas).
- Could: Things you might do if you have time left over

This easy substitution is revealing. You can enter the day knowing what is most truly valuable.

Another powerful approach is the Eisenhower Urgent-Important Matrix. Let's be realistic here. You receive an invitation to a 6 PM Zoom web conference and a separate invitation to a 6 PM call with your independent contractor client. Do you go to that one?

The client call is an absolute priority—it affects revenue and trust. That's priority number one.

Priorities have nothing to do with doing more—they have to do with whether it's worth your energy.

The Art of Ruthless Boundaries - Drawing the Line Between Job & Dream:-

Boundaries are everything. Without them, your job, hustle, and personal life can blur into a mess. One of the most challenging things side-hustlers must get is that time fences are egocentric, but they must be. Otherwise, your life, day job, and business will all be something until you crash.

Let's say your boss has a habit of sending work to you at 6 PM, and you have dedicated your side business to nights. This breaks your rhythm. This is what you tell them:

"Happy to do it if it's urgent—otherwise I'll do it first thing tomorrow morning."

Respectful, professional, and polite.

And when relatives find you at home in the evening and assume that you are available for errands or socialising, let them know:

"I'm doing my project after office hours—it is not 'spare time' but work I've taken up."

Weekend planning is your hack. Set Saturday and Sunday as startup sprint days. Schedule some focused hours for your business, then leave the rest free to chill, run errands, or meet up with friends.

Keep in mind that you're not working harder to work just to get here and become stagnant. You're creating a life where your passion receives the same level of attention.

Time Blocking & Focus Zones

Forget robotic planners and colour-coded schedules. Productivity isn't about filling every minute—it's about knowing your best minutes. Most people aren't tired because they don't have enough time; they're exhausted because they're trying to be productive when they're at their most lethargic. Welcome to the world of energy mapping.

Begin by monitoring your natural energy cycle for a few days. Is it best at 6 a.m. or do you have a second wind at 9 p.m.? Chart your highs and lows in energy, not trying to create an unrealistic 6 a.m. "miracle routine" that you will have abandoned by Wednesday.

Take Ashok, who works full-time for a consulting firm. His thinking mode is active after dinner, so he spends 9:30 p.m. to midnight working on features for his ed-tech app rather than fighting it. He gets his low-effort administrative tasks (e.g., emails) done during his afternoon dip.

Your energy is your secret weapon. Align your most important tasks with your most substantial hours—not someone else's "miracle routine."

The Sunday Sync- Up – Your Secret Weapon

Sunday isn't just a day—it's a sanctuary. Envision Sunday as your board meeting—no corporate speak—just you, your mind, and a pen.

Begin with a 10-minute journal dump. Ask: What surprised me this week? What uplifted me? What did I sidestep, and why? You'll be surprised how easily answers flow when not typing into a planner app.

Then, attempt goal stacking. Choose three:

- One stretch goal that challenges you
- One sustainable goal that sustains you
- One soothing goal that relaxes you

Example

- Stretch: Make one new client pitch video
- Sustain: Prepare three workdays' worth of food.
- Soothe: Sunday night, read only, no screens.

Lastly, look at your calendar—not to schedule but to fight it. Are appointments made to accommodate someone else's calendar or yours?

This will take under 30 minutes to add to your routine. But it can reshape a week so it serves you, not just your obligations.

Tools and Strategies That Work

Beyond Notion and Trello—What Works for You

Don't waste brainpower on things that can run themselves. If a task isn't your passion or doesn't require your personal touch, automate it. Using Notion, ClickUp, or the latest AI planner,

Productivity is about consistency, not trendiness. One entrepreneur scaled her business on an Excel sheet, while another built a system through WhatsApp reminders. Work with what suits *you*. It's not about the trendiest tool; it's about what sticks.

If you're visual, you'll likely dislike endless lists. Try using sticky notes on a whiteboard, wall calendar, or plain old sketch maps to organise your week.

You'll love apps like Todoist or even the good old bullet journaling method if you're a checklist nerd. You enjoy checking things off and seeing the weight of accomplishment in your mind's eye.

If you're a verbal processor, record your tasks and talk them through with a voice note app. Sometimes just saying it out loud clears the fog.

Automate the Mundane

There are only two valid reasons to do something manually: because it's your favourite thing or because it requires your special attention. Anything else? Automate it.

Begin with the basics:

- Emails: Automatically tag client emails with filters or enable canned responses in Gmail.
- Finances: Automatically log expenses using tools such as Zoho Books or QuickBooks.
- Reminders: Use Google Calendar to set reminders for paying bills, following up on calls, or practising drills.

Then progress to more sophisticated (but still user-friendly) tools:

- Zapier: Automate complicated multi-step workflows. For example, Zapier greets you and updates your Notion CRM whenever you receive a form submission.
- IFTTT: "If This, Then That" allows you to link apps according to rules. For example, you can back up all your Instagram photos to Google Drive.
- Google Calendar hacks: Colour-code work, business, and personal on different calendar colours. Share the top ones only with the team or family.

You're liberated by automation from mundane decisions. And the fewer decisions you make daily, the more space is available for the big ones that expand your business.

Delegating Without a Team

You don't need a large staff to start delegating; you just need to think and be flexible. Don't confuse delegation with headcount, but rather with loading the work out in terms of thinking and adaptable arrangements.

Begin by delegating work to interns—students willing to gain experience. Promote it to them as a project-learning exercise. You receive help, they receive real-life experience.

The golden rule? Pare down whatever is repeatable, learnable, and time-consuming. Don't do it all. Do just the essentials.

Productivity is not hustling 24/7

Being busy is not something to be proud of. And for entrepreneurs, identifying activity with progress is a dangerous delusion. Actual productivity is getting the job done well, not harder. Find out the 80/20 Principle: 80% of results are caused by 20% of efforts.

Assume you have a candle business. You sell 10 different fragrances, but sales data indicate that 80% of your revenue is generated by the two best-selling products alone. Why waste money marketing the rest? Market more of the ones that already do the job.

Apply the same principle to marketing platforms, networking, and client work.

You will be efficient and unmovable when you cease attempting to do everything and begin focusing on high-leverage activities.

The "Deep Work" Advantage - where Magic happens

You don't need more hours. You need better quality hours.

Deep work is unbroken, focused time devoted to the most crucial tasks, such as writing, planning, or creation. With a 9-to-5 job, one focused hour of deep work daily can outperform four superficial hours.

So, how do you create deep work pockets?

- Environment design: Engage your brain with a physical or symbolic ritual. Light a candle, wear headphones, and close the door: small signals, giant impact.
- The Phone: Put the phone somewhere else or in another drawer—out of sight, out of mind.
- Focus playlists: Cycles of instrumentals, ambient soundscapes, and lo-fi hip-hop beats—create a playlist that serves as your brain's cue to "go time." Your brain will eventually associate the tunes with work mode.
- Workspace rituals: It may be getting your workspace out the night before or having coffee at the same workstation. Don't

underestimate the power of repetition to drive that laser-like focus.
- Consistent effort, just 60 minutes a day, grows exponentially quicker.

Overcoming Procrastination and Burnout

Why We Put It Off

Business owners attribute procrastination to laziness. Nine out of ten times, it's a hidden fear.

You're not putting off the task; you're putting off what the task does to you: making you lose, confused, or uncertain.

Try this the next time you're scrolling or stalling

- Confusion: I'm unsure of my next steps.
- Fear: Am I going to be afraid it's not good enough?
- Boredom: Am I simply not experiencing the task?

The moment you recognise the emotion behind the resistance, it's easy to overcome. If you're confused, break the project down into manageable steps. If you're afraid, remind yourself you must write a horrible first draft. Add music, a timer, or a reward if you're apathetic.

Procrastination is not a weakness—it's a sign. Take one real step at a time.

Motivation Through Movement

When you freeze up there in your head, move.

Entrepreneurs hate the feeling of having to "tough it out," but burnout increases when one disregards the body. Body movement increases focus, re-tunes the nervous system, and generates new ideas.

No gym membership required -Instead, do these:

- 10-minute dance breaks between calls.
- Phone-free evening strolls, by yourself with your head.
- Take a chair stretch or do yoga during your Pomodoro breaks.
- Power naps and sleep hygiene—no deadline will beat a tired mind.

Confident and successful founders attribute their productivity to exercise routines and movement. A fashion designer starts the morning with sun salutations. A copywriter brings his legs into a squat while papers spin on his desk. A tech founder takes a walk when he has a 1:1 meeting scheduled on his calendar.

Your body is your initial productivity asset. Treat it as your partner, not an afterthought.

The "Micro-Win" Habit

Instead of waking up to an enormous to-do list, use micro-wins. They are teeny-tiny but super potent actions that move your business without draining your energy.

Examples of Micro-Wins:

- Respond to 2 cold emails or lead emails.
- Publish 1 Instagram photo or product photo.
- Come up with three content or product names.
- Read a customer complaint or yesterday's sales.
- Read two pages of a business book at lunch.

They'll feel too small to count, but add them up over 30 days, and you'll have quantifiable forward progress.

Tip: Replace your "To-Do List" with a "Done List."

Write down what you accomplished at the end of each day. This will help you get in the rhythm of enjoying action instead of begrudging perfection.

The Done List is also a measure of momentum, reminding you on slow days how much you have already accomplished.

Burnout Is Not a Badge of Honour - it's an alarm.

The key takeaway: burnout is not something to brag about. It's an indicator.

Side-hustle founders burn both ends of the candle—and the wick in between. But running on fumes leads to regrettable choices, from deals that fall through to relationships that end in disappointment.

Early Warning Signs of Burnout

- You're resentful of your side hustle or your 9–5.
- You're short-fusing with others increasingly.
- You get yourself ready to work, and your head just... refuses to.
- You have no idea when you last had a day off.

If that's what happens, just stop. Don't attempt to push through; instead, gradually back off.

Recovery Protocol:

- Reset habits: Take the weekend and do nothing. Then, taper back to a less desperate pace.
- Get a friend or mentor to speak with. Burnout is often not evident until someone shines a light on it.
- Cut the non-essential tasks: Ask yourself, "What if I didn't do this?" You'd be surprised at how much unnecessary fluff there is.

Always remember - Your business deserves the best you, not your drained self.

Final Reflection + Habit Builder

Take a moment and build your beat with intention.

Reflection Questions:

- Where is my time leaking? (e.g., scrolling, meetings, perfectionism)
- What are three things that make my business thrive?
- What is one thing that I will condition myself to for the next 30 days?
- Now, keep moving, apply what you've learned, and create a routine that functions.

Custom Routine Builder (Template)

Time Block	Weekdays	Weekends
Morning (6-9 AM)	e.g., Walk + 1 creative hour	e.g., Brunch, rest, light planning
Midday (9-5 PM)	Full-time job	Deep work on business (2–3 hours max)

Evening (5-9 PM)	e.g., Business admin, learning, or content	e.g., Social time, hobby, or self-care
Night (9-11 PM)	Wind down, journal, reset space	Watch, read, or reflect

> Pro Tip: Choose *two days a week* when business tasks take priority and one full day when nothing is planned. Recovery *is* a task.

Visual Tracker: Balance at a Glance

Create four colour-coded boxes on a calendar:

- ▨Job
- ▧Business
- ▨Rest
- ▧Growth (Learning, Skill-building)

At the end of each day, colour the box that dominated. At the end of the week, check for imbalance. If red and yellow are missing, your future self is being neglected. If green and blue dominate, you might be overworking.

Chapter 9: Rising Stronger: Turning Challenges into Triumphs

Dealing with Failure and Setbacks:

The Emotional Reality of Failure

Failure isn't just financial. It's emotional. It's the silence that follows an ambitious launch that flops. It's walking into your workspace and feeling like you're trespassing in your dream. It's returning a customer's call, knowing they're angry, and not having a solution.

Ask any entrepreneur—not the ones on magazine covers, but the ones still figuring out margins—and they'll tell you:. Failure isn't the exception—it's the initiation.

" Ayeshas' cafe- Ayesha's café didn't fail because of rent hikes alone. It failed because she served chai with her grandmother's recipes, but forgot to charge enough to keep the lights on.
Failure is your business's autopsy report. Don't look away—study it. The clues to your comeback are in the incision marks.

Coping Mechanisms That Work

No map to come back from a broken dream. But you carry coping capital that allows you to bounce back—not intact, maybe, but resilient. Resilience isn't about perfection. It's about adaptation.

- Journaling
  You script your own story before the world writes one for you. What did you do? What did you do successfully? What are you never doing again?
- Therapy or Mentorship
  On other days, there is someone with you who excels at it. Ask what goes on behind the scenes. If you don't have money for therapy, talk to a mentor or fellow entrepreneur. Shame melts when shared.
- Peer Support
  Stay in founder networks or even WhatsApp groups for entrepreneurs where you live. Most aren't "killing it." They're just struggling to get their head above water. And that's reassuring.
- Take a Break Without Shame
  You don't bounce back in 10 days. Doing nothing is doing—clarity, energy, courage.

Exercise: A Letter to Your Future Self

Write from where you are in failure. Write to your future self:

- What went down and how it made you feel
- What you're scared of losing
- What you wish they've constructed from here

Start with:
"I don't know where this will take me, but here's what I've learned so far..."

The "Fail, Feel, Fix" Process

There is a 3-step process that most successful business people fall into way too often:

- Fail
  Admit what failed. Be specific. Don't beat around the bush.
- Feel
  Let yourself grieve the you who did take risks. Cry if that is what you need to do. Leave if you have to. But don't numb yourself out of existence.
- Fix
  Return with clarity. Think, redo, and try again. Restoring is not redoing history—it is only constructing your next attempt.

"Failure provided space for growth—not a business, but me."

Building Resilience and Mental Toughness:

Reality On Resilience

- Perseverance is repeating the same thing repeatedly.
- Resilience is knowing how to turn back, turn around, or continue.

- Blind determination says, "I'll push till I break."
- Actual resilience demands, "I'll adjust to survive without breaking."

Indications That You're Getting Mentally Tough:

- You make decisions without considering what other people will do with them.
- You see rejection as being otherwise directed.
- You let go of the need to hold your value hostage to approval.
- You no longer feel driven to prove yourself so much.

Resilience is covert. It does not scream in TED Talks. It appears when you pitch and stress out, when you sleep 8 hours instead of tossing and turning all night, and when you terminate a toxic client.

Tools to Develop Inner Resilience

- Mindfulness
  5 minutes a day. No phones. Just breathe. Observe thoughts, don't judge them, but notice how loud your mind is.
- Stoicism
  Old school plain philosophy. Excellent epigraph: "You can't control what happens to you. You can only control how you respond." Write that somewhere you will see it.
- Breathing Techniques
  Breathe in for 4 seconds, hold for 4 seconds, and breathe out for 6 seconds. Do this until your hands release and your head returns to normal.

Entrepreneur Story: Pritam, D2C Fashion Brand

Pritam pitched 37. No one said yes. On the 38th pitch, he received five hundred thousand in investment. "I made a ritual," he says. "Each 'no,' I'd write, have comfort food, and take tomorrow off."
He wasn't addicted to the hustle. He was playing for keeps.

Resilience Mini Workbook

Exercise: What do I believe about my resilience?

- "I am someone who bounces back."
- "When I am feeling overwhelmed, I typically..."
- "What I would prefer to do differently when faced with setbacks is..."

Table: Resilience Moments in My Life

The moment I struggled	What I did	What it taught me
____________________	___________	___________________
____________________	___________	___________________
____________________	___________	___________________

Let this table remind you that you've made it through 100% of your worst days so far. You're already resilient. Now you're learning to make it conscious.

Say to yourself, "I am not a machine. I am a monsoon—sometimes wild, sometimes still, but always replenishing myself."

Learning from Mistakes:

From Embarrassment to Insight

Entrepreneurs don't regret mistakes—they respect them. Every entrepreneur has at least one story that starts with "I wish I'd known better." That feeling—of missteps, miscalculations, or outright failure—can be hard to sit with. But over time, it becomes the root of wisdom.

Consider, for example, Zarish, who started an organic soap business. She bought the initial bulk order from a vendor she had discovered online without tasting the stuff. When the order finally arrived, 300 of them were mouldy. She had already exhausted all her cash and lost it all.

She cried, contemplated cancelling, and then got up. She discovered that one should try first before making a bulk purchase, all to be signed and dated in writing, and never hasten an order. Her second order was a success. She still considers the first one "the most expensive lesson she ever bought."

Mistakes aren't detours—they're tuition fees for wisdom. Mistakes don't mean you failed. They tell you that you're learning something shortcuts can't teach.

Create Your Feedback Loop

You won't ever trip—you will get up having tripped. You can have a feedback loop for yourself and learn from each fall.
This is how:

- Write it down. If anything goes wrong, don't just plough on. Spend ten minutes writing down what went wrong, straight and plain.
- Ask the right questions. What did I believe that wasn't true? What part of this was within my control?
- Try again. Don't overcorrect. Simply move one thing, try it out, and see what changes.

Even keeping a "Mistake Journal" where you write down lessons as they occur leaves room for regret to look back on. You're not just learning, you're writing down your progress.

Observing Progress

Progress doesn't require a graph. It requires a glance at your before and after.

Remember that one mistake you made in the beginning—a careless decision, a poor hire, a lacklustre launch. Now, consider how you'd replicate the same scenario today.

That room? That's where you started.

You're no longer there, but you're still trying to resolve the same conundrum. Experience had modified your approach, even though you didn't notice it.

Staying Motivated When Things Go Wrong:

It's Not Discipline—It's Vision

Your list of things to do will sometimes gather dust, accomplishing nothing. There is minimal momentum, no sales, and nothing is going anywhere.

This is where all the other so-called experts talk about discipline, but rarely entrepreneurs. It's never a matter of force. It's a matter of clarity of vision—reminding yourself why you did it in the first place.

One of the company's founders described how she persisted during six months of no progress, not so much because she was self-motivated as because she could so obviously imagine her brand on every store shelf. She was energised by the vision when progress constantly eluded her.

Vision need not be heroic. It just needs to be precise. Whatever you need to create, that you want to reach out and touch, or that freedom you need—hold that in your mind each day.

Mood-Lifters That Work

Motivation is not a matter of psyching yourself up—it's a matter of anchoring yourself in what matters.

Here are a few doable rituals that can boost your mood on tough days:

- Work with a companion. Working quietly with a companion or coworker nearby can create a communal energy that helps maintain your focus.
- Build a ritual. Begin your workday with the same tune, the same cup of coffee, or the same five-minute investment. Rituals create rhythm, and rhythm creates momentum.
- Listen to audio affirmations. Tape yourself reading your goals, future vision, or what you're passionate about in this firm. Listen while walking, cleaning the house, or at night. It's absurd initially, but it becomes second nature after a while.

Don't grit your teeth when it's hard. Instead, use rhythm, routine, and a dash of fun to carry you through.

The Motivation Poster & Circle

Make something real—something still speaking to you even on not-so-good days when you don't feel like listening.

Put the following on a sticky note or poster:

- "I'll show up, even if I don't feel ready."
- Then, underneath, write:
- One business goal that is important to you
- One thing you've already done that didn't come easily
- One person for whom you're doing this

Place it on your desk, in front of your mirror, or in your journal. Then start building your network—not networking, but flotation.

Name:

- One person who'll call you every Friday.
- One person who won't flinch at calling BS on your excuses.
- One person who keeps you reminded of how far you've gone.

These are your motivation anchors. When their spark loses its flame, they can re-ignite yours.

Traps of First-Time Entrepreneurs:

The Top 5 Traps to Avoid

Starting a business may be fun. However, fun has a way of getting clouded by good judgment, and that is how most first-time entrepreneurs avoid getting themselves trapped. These are some of the most common ones:

- Taking on too many employees too quickly.
  Bhavana began a sustainable stationery business and employed a full-time operations lead, marketer, and designer within the first three months. However, her burn rate skyrocketed before she could scale her revenue, so she had to lay off some staff and scale more intentionally, starting with freelancers.

- Underpricing to "get into the market."
  Sajid began selling his cost-plus line of hand-stitched shoes. He believed he was building customer loyalty, but after finally pricing up, customers deserted him. He had to rebrand and retarget to create a more profitable customer base.

- Failure to conduct market research.
  Mohit, a fitness coach, created a whole course based on what she believed her clients required. Three people signed up. After posting a basic 5-question Google Form, she finally

discovered that her clients were seeking brief routines, not heaps of theory.

- Tunnel vision for the idea, not the client.
  One of the founders created a rural payment app without leaving the village. It was overengineered, the text was too small to read, and there was little to no take-up. He returned, conversed with users, and did it all again—this time from scratch—but with them.

- The inability to do everything yourself.
  Mehul was the classic solo founder, designer, marketer, developer, and customer support. He burned out in six months. He grew faster and happier once he asked for help, even from interns and his network.

Mistakes aren't signs you're failing. They're just signs you're going fast without a map. Every founder makes some. The smart ones slow down, reroute, and keep driving.
Always remember - your business is a ship. Where are the leaks? What's the one patch that would keep you afloat

How to Get Rid Of What You Can

You cannot eliminate all errors, but you can eliminate the avoidable ones. It is like installing speed breakers on the road instead of waiting for your demise.

Some winning habits of business founders that bring revenue are listed below:

- Customer pulse checks. Burn simple, raw questions before seeding anything in the earth. "Would you pay for this?" is a better sieve than "Do you like this?"
- Mentor moments. A 15-minute voice note from someone 2 years ahead of you can save you 2 months of guess-and-check.
- Test lean. Make the duct-tape version of your product first. If 10 won't test the bootstrapped one, 100 won't buy the high-end one.

Try this journal prompt:

"The mistake I'm most afraid of is ___."

"If it did happen, I would ___."

Write it. You won't fall—you're just getting ready to stand up if you do.

Red Flags & Emotional Cues

Burnout and failure won't catch us off guard one day. We generally do have warning signs--we're just not paying attention.

Some emotional warning signs to begin looking out for here:

- "When I feel rushed, I cut corners and later regret it."
- "When I feel doubtful, I delay key decisions."

- "When I'm burned out, I quit on things so I won't get in trouble."

Use these as warning signs; don't ignore them. Ask yourself: Is this how I want to build my business?

The Importance of Self-Care & Work-Life Balance:

What Burnout Looks Like

It doesn't always appear to be a meltdown. Burnout prefers to creep up on you:

- You start sleeping worse.
- You're not even thrilled about good news.
- You start disliking Mondays, Tuesdays and Wednesdays.
- You're seriously sick but don't know why.

Let's take the example.

Moiz was becoming more authoritarian. He battled insomnia, avoided meals, and worked day and night. He fainted on stage during a product launch and took a 3-month break.

It's not whether you're going to rest—it's when. Getting it sooner is a strength. Waiting until you're burned out is defeat.

Getting Self-Care onto the CEO Agenda

Self-care isn't indulgence. It's maintenance. Like lubricating a machine, self-care also lubricates your brain and body.

This is how you schedule it in so it can't be bumped off:

- Schedule an appointment for it first. Whatever it is to you—your gym time, weekly therapy session, or no-screening night before bed—schedule it as a non-rescheduled appointment.
- Name it. What gets you feeling fabulous, not just crossing things off? Long baths? Music walks? Timer-less cooking? Schedule it.

Make a template of this exercise:

"How do I care for myself like I'm a person who counts?"

Not once a year. Daily.

Your business will not appreciate you if you burn out, but it will soar when you're full of energy, enthusiasm, and emotional equilibrium.

Your Weekly Self-Care Planner

Complete this easy-to-use planning template on Sundays:

- Something I'll do for my body:
- Something I'll do for my peace:
- Something I'll establish as a boundary:

- Something kind I'll do without apology:

And last, read this wall of wisdom when you are reminding yourself of your value:

"Rest is not idleness."

"Your business is a reflection of your energy."

"If you burned out building it, it wasn't worth it."

"Success at the cost of your health isn't success."

You are not your output. You are your presence. Treat it kindly.

Write it down. **Your future self will thank you.**

Chapter 10: The Leap Forward: A Call to Action

The Shift from Builder to Guide: Alchemy of Mentorship

Along each entrepreneur's journey, the attention will shift away from constructing your dream toward helping others build theirs. It's not away from growth—it's a subset of it.

Because you've ridden out the storm of the mysterious, the burn-out of all-nighters and early risings, and the thrill of infinitesimally small wins, you're optimally positioned to usher someone new into the battlefield. Mentorship isn't a detour—it's the hidden garden where your battles bloom into another's breakthroughs. Always remember, " *You are no longer just a sculptor of dreams—you are the torchbearer lighting the way for others.* "

Why does it matter to them?

Hardworking, successful business owners likely suffer from impostor syndrome, self-doubt, or alienation. A few words of wisdom from a "been there" friend may be more valuable than any YouTube channel and blog post ever could be.

Why it matters to you:

Mentorship shapes your thoughts into a more concrete definition. It forces you to set boundaries on your path, own your narrative, and stick to your fundamentals. And it reminds you again and again of your "why"—something much too easy to forget in the growth process.

Imagine planting seeds in another person's garden while enriching your roots.

Casual Mentorships That Make an Impact

You don't necessarily need a program, curriculum, or even the term "mentor" to qualify.

Take David, for example, who began mentoring through direct messages on Twitter. A person who aspires to be a fintech entrepreneur asked him a question about venture capitalists. Something light became every other week's voice messages. The same mentee raised capital two years later and attributes his turnaround to David.

Tips on how to start mentoring casually:

- Answer purposefully to DMs
- Share real behind-the-scenes anecdotes.
- Volunteer to provide feedback on a pitch deck or product concept
- Send voice messages rather than marathon Zooms.
- Let people ask you questions.

Mentorship doesn't begin with, "Let me mentor you." It starts with: "What are you working on these days?"

Designated /Structured Mentorship—Workshops, Calls, and Check-Ins

Designated mentorship is the answer to making a more significant impact in a repeatable and targeted way. You don't need to be a half-time coach; all you need is a plan and an intention.

Some ways of doing that:

- 1:1 Coaching: Time-limited offers like a "3-call sprint" or "45-minute business review."
- Community Groups: Private Telegram groups, Slack groups, or newsletters where you answer questions and post announcements.
- Micro-Courses: Brief, interactive courses like "Pricing your freelance proposal" or "Product-market fit 101."

Ambreen, the founder of a sustainable lifestyle brand, hosts a monthly "Founder Roundtable"—a two-hour Zoom call for five new founders to discuss challenges and solutions. She doesn't sell anything. It's simply structure, support, and solidarity. Members have started podcasts and retail stores and discovered cooperation here.

Structural mentorship doesn't need scale, but presence.

Common Mistakes to Avoid as a Mentor

Good intentions can trap you if you're not careful to avoid the following pitfalls:

1. Talking more than listening.
Not all mentees have to be "fixed." They may need a while to listen to themselves think. Ask first before advising.

2. Superimposing your journey over theirs.
Your journey was exactly what you needed, but it's not theirs. Your talent, networking, and market timing are all distinct variables.

3. Over-investing.
You don't need to be available 24/7 to be valuable. If done well, even a 15-minute touch base every few weeks can move mountains.

Mentoring is not about perfection—it's about being intentional. Set your ego aside, keep an open mind, and ensure your energy is genuine.

Mentoring Without Burnout

Successful hacks for managing mentoring:

- Establish boundaries: "I have two mentorship calls per month. Do you want to get on the waitlist?"

- Use voice notes or Zoom videos to give feedback without live calls.
- Have group calls rather than 1:1s to save time and establish peer support.
- Establish office hours: Choose a Friday afternoon or Sunday morning when you can spend a few minutes on quick consults.

Reuse this script:
"Hi! I'm happy to help you. I have short 15-minute voice note sessions or group calls on the last Saturday of every month. Would that work for you?"

Mentorship, done well and with boundaries, is a gift and not a drain. Be present when you can. Say what is true when you can't. And trust that even a little bit of wisdom, given freely, can change someone's life forever.

Creating a Legacy- The Ripple You Never See

“Legacy isn’t carved in marble—it’s etched in the quiet moments that outlive you."

Legacy doesn't require a statue, a bestseller, or a viral video. It just requires intention.
We think of legacy in significant terms: billion-dollar exits, national recognition, or lasting impact. What if your legacy is:

- The intern who launched her empire because you said, *"Why not you?"*
- The stranger who found courage in your midnight blog post.

Let's dissect it:

1. Personal Legacy
How you interact with the individuals closest and dearest to you, such as your family, employees, or mentees, and the lasting energy you leave behind in the room.
2. Industry Legacy
The innovations, templates, and concepts that you bring to your organisation. Whether you execute a new procedure or cast aside the old model, you define the rules for how the next generation gets the job done.
3. Community Legacy
The hands you lift without waiting for applause. "Legacy begins with daily decisions, not magic."

Industry Influence- Be the Voice of Industry

You don't need a title—just a voice, courage to speak, and generosity to share it.

How to create industry influence:

- Write publicly: Share your takeaway through blogs, newsletters, or LinkedIn articles.

- Speak at events: Participate in webinars or panels to represent your niche and establish your expertise.
- Open-source your tools: Develop templates, checklists, or guides that one can implement.

Example:

Rimsha, a socially conscious fashion entrepreneur, observed some of the freelance designers struggling in vendor negotiations. She set it free on Instagram. Overnight, she became the unsung hero of freelance designers.

Industry influence isn't gatekeeping your genius. It's being the businessperson you wished you'd be when you started.

Community- The Art of Rising Together, where you grew up

Your roots are your compass. Dig deeper where you're planted."

Some actual examples:

- Mehrab, the software billionaire, funds coding camps for local teens every summer.
- Neha, a home baker, provides free Saturday workshops to underprivileged girls.
- Henry, a craft brew businessman, sources raw ingredients from small-scale farmers and provides credit on each bottle label.

None of them is newsworthy on their face. But to the lives you touch, they're permanent.

Impact tip: You don't have to write a CSR plan. You just have a kind heart.
Always Remember - *Giving back doesn't dilute your mission; it enriches it.*

Building Values Into Your Business

Your business is a vehicle. But what fuels it—money or meaning—is your choice. What you choose to fuel it.

Embedding values means:

- Pay workers fairly, even when nobody is looking.
- Make websites and content accessible.
- Choosing eco-conscious packaging.

Ask yourself:

"Who benefits here?" And are my shareholders the only ones?
"Who gets left behind?" "Are my services accessible by class, gender, or ability?"

Legacy isn't a secondary side-mission. It's how your business breathes when nobody's looking.

Reflection prompt

"What do I want to be remembered for, not by strangers, but by the people I know?"

“What am I doing today that will allow me to live into that memory?”

Real legacy is not a blare of trumpets in one's life, but a quiet, persistent echo of your values over time.

Reflecting Is Not a Distraction—It’s Fuel

You did something. It might still be just starting, learning how to stand on its own, but you did that.

Entrepreneurs often rush past their successes, chasing the next opportunity. But reflection is the refuel you need to go further. Growth isn’t just money. It’s clarity. Calm. Confidence. Courage.

Rituals of Celebration

"Success is a desert if you don’t pause to drink the mirage."

A celebration doesn't have to be marked by confetti and thunderous applause. It can be subtle, purposeful, and deeply personal.

And these are some examples of how entrepreneurs have put celebration into practice in their lives:

- Solo Retreats: One founder takes himself away for a weekend every quarter to write, reflect, and renew in the mountains—no agenda, no email, just silence.
- Gratitude Letters: After a phenomenal year, one startup team makes time to sit down and write thank-you letters by hand to all those who helped them along the way, including mentors, customers, and interns.
- Giving Back: Some founders commemorate business milestones by supporting a favourite cause or mentoring a newcomer.

What's your way?

Your celebration can be:

- Taking your family out to dinner.
- Sharing your story in a voice note to your future self.
- Printing your first invoice and framing it.
- Lighting a candle and saying, "I'm proud of myself."

Rituals make our progress real. Don't skip the joy.

The Power of Storytelling: Your Journey

Your story is powerful—not in how you lived it, but in how you share it. "Your stumbles are someone else's survival guide."

Sharing your entrepreneurial journey helps:

- You distil and solidify your development.
- Others don't quite feel so solitary in their struggle.
- Your younger self, through a listener's ears, gets heard.

Setting the Next Mountain

So what's next?
Success can sometimes feel like a dead-end when it should feel like a launchpad. That's why the next question is key:

"What still excites me?"
"What would feel scary and new right now?"

These questions aren't about scale. They're about growing. Growth can mean expanding your business, healing, mentoring, exploring, or pivoting.

Framework to keep momentum alive:

- Learn – like a curious child.
- Build – like a rebel artist.
- Teach –like the mentor you needed at 3 a.m.
- Leap - like the ground will rise to meet you.

The Last Call to Action

You've come this far.

Now, close out this chapter with these on-purpose actions:

- **Mission Statement:** *"I am doing_____ because I believe_____*
- Service + Dream: Mentor one soul. Reclaim your Sundays. Start the thing.
- Letter to Future You: "Dear Me in 5 Years

"

Expert Opinion - Pick up the pen. The world needs your story—unfinished, unfiltered, utterly yours.

Chapter 11: Conclusion- Giving Back: Building Your Legacy and Empowering Others

Most entrepreneurial journeys kick off with a whisper. That whisper is of curiosity.

"What if I tried something different?"

"What if I created something of my own?"

As an employee, you learn to appreciate the safety net—steady paychecks, predictable routines, and defined roles. There's a framework that supports you. But for many, this framework can also feel like an invisible barrier. Over time, you might start to feel trapped, not out of ingratitude, but because you sense there's more inside you just waiting to come out.

This stage is filled with emotional contradictions.

You might experience:

Fear of leaving: What if I fail?

Guilt: Shouldn't I be grateful for what I have?

Self-doubt: Do I even have what it takes?

Excitement, buried under pressure: What if this works?

This is the internal tug-of-war that happens before any decision is made.

Your ambition simmers quietly, often misunderstood, even by those closest to you. You find yourself toying with side projects at night, tuning into business podcasts during lunch breaks, and daydreaming about emails that start with, "I'm writing to resign."

The beginning isn't a leap; it's more of a stir.

And if you've felt this way, you're already ahead of the game.

The Shift Begins

There comes a moment—a conversation, a burnout, a random post online—that makes you think:

"Maybe I could..."

That's not just a fleeting thought. That's your inner entrepreneur knocking at the door.

This chapter of your journey marks the beginning of a significant shift. You don't just quit your job on a whim. Instead, you begin to gain clarity. You start exploring:

What do I want to create?

Who do I want to serve?

What am I willing to sacrifice for this?

You discover that Entrepreneurship isn't recklessness. It's building a bridge while walking on it—one plank of courage at a time. This book has guided you through those early stages:

- Starting without all the answers.

- Researching while battling self-doubt.
- Taking your first business step even when you're not entirely confident.

The change isn't sudden. It's gradual, purposeful, and deeply personal. But once it starts, you find yourself transformed in ways you never expected.

Learning and Building

The learning curve is steep, but it's exhilarating. You come to realise that being an entrepreneur requires a whole new set of skills that your previous job never asked for:

- Managing your time when no deadlines are looming over you.
- Finding deep focus despite endless distractions.
- Delegating tasks without a conventional team to rely on.

You dive into learning through trial and error. You figure out how to:

- Set clear boundaries with clients.
- Sell your ideas without coming off as pushy.
- Create even when no one is watching.

And gradually, you start to see those milestones pop up:

- Your first client, even if the pay was less than ideal.
- Your first rejection, which stung more than you anticipated.
- Your first success, which felt more rewarding than any job review.

These moments aren't just business achievements; they're markers of your identity. You begin to see yourself not just as someone with a side gig, but as a person who is genuinely building something meaningful.

The Inner Shift

The most significant changes aren't what others can see—they're the emotional ones.

You start confronting what you used to shy away from:

- The fear of judgment.
- The shame that comes from making mistakes.
- The emotional ups and downs of unpredictable results.

Yet, with each hurdle, you gain something invaluable: resilience.

You begin to practice:

- Self-kindness on the tough days.
- Finding motivation through your vision, not just external approval.
- Grit that shines without the need for glamour.

True entrepreneurs develop emotional maturity, not just strategies. While you can't control external metrics, you can control your ability to rebuild, adapt, and push forward.

From Employee to an Entrepreneur

One day, without realising it, your mindset shifts. You stop thinking like an employee dabbling in a side hustle—you see yourself as a **founder**.

Not because you've made millions, but because you've chosen to own your decisions.

Entrepreneurship isn't about chasing prestige; it's about designing a life **on your terms**.

The path from employee to entrepreneur isn't a straight shot. It's a winding journey filled with action, reflection, setbacks, and growth. But now, you're not waiting for someone to pick you. You've already chosen to pursue this path, and that changes everything.

You Are Not Behind

If you're reading this and thinking, "I should've started five years ago," or "I'm too late to the game," or "Everyone else is ahead," take a deep breath. You're not behind; you're on your journey.

Entrepreneurship doesn't come with a timer; it comes with a spark. Some discover it at 22, while others find it at 42, and both paths are entirely valid. The pressure to be "early" can often lead to hasty decisions and superficial efforts. What truly matters is whether you're building something meaningful—something that lasts.

Comparison can be one of the biggest traps you'll encounter. Online, you might see 19-year-olds launching apps and 30-year-olds securing millions in funding. But behind those headlines are countless hours of hard work, false starts, and late-night doubts.

Always Remember: Entrepreneurship isn't a race; it's a **journey**. You're not late. You're just beginning.

Courage Over Confidence

Here's a secret: confidence isn't the key to success—courage is. Courage says, "Let's give it a shot." Confidence arrives later, whispering, "You did it."

Grow Without Burning Bridges-

Quitting everything isn't the only path. The fact is that many entrepreneurs build gradually, sustainably: A design on a Sunday, a blog post during lunch, or A pitch sent from a café

These moments of quiet progress are just as powerful as dramatic launches. Honour your current job—it funds your dream. Grow your side project with love and patience. You don't have to burn the boat to reach new shores.

The Antidote to Naysayers -

Not everyone will understand your vision. Some will question it: they might say:

"That sounds risky."

"You're not the business type."

"Is this even worth your time?"

Sometimes, the loudest voice of doubt will be your own. Here's a reminder: Your "why" doesn't need any validation. You don't need applause; you need momentum.

Clarity isn't something you wait for, but something that grows through messy action. The more you create, the more precise your vision becomes. The more you try, the more you'll trust yourself. Let the scepticism drive you forward, not hold you back.

You're not out to convince the world. You're simply proving it to yourself, one courageous step at a time.

You're Already Ahead Than You Think

If you've made it to this point, you're not a dreamer anymore—you're a doer.

That's rare.

Most people never get this far. Revisit your journal. Reread the notes you scribbled. Take just one small action today—send that email, build that page, or call that mentor.

Small acts compound. They create waves. Don't wait for perfection. Start now. Momentum comes from action, not perfection.

Your Next Move Doesn't Need to Be Big

Starting can feel daunting when you're picturing a grand launch, a viral campaign, or quitting your job all at once. But honestly, your first step doesn't have to be anything spectacular—it just needs to be genuine. Each small step declares, "I'm doing this." Your empire doesn't need to start with fireworks. It begins with one clear decision.

Anchor Yourself With Why

As you embark on this journey, you'll encounter moments of doubt, fatigue, and distractions. What will keep you grounded isn't a strategy—it's your purpose.

Ask yourself: "Why do I want this life?"

It could be as simple as:

- "I want freedom over my time."

- "I want to create something my family will be proud of."

- "I want to help people like me feel seen."

Write it down and place it somewhere you'll see it often—on your lock screen, pinned to your mirror, or taped to your laptop. This single line will serve as your emotional compass, reminding you who you're doing this for when the path ahead gets foggy.

You don't need a detailed business plan at this time.
You just need a compelling reason to take the next step.

Support, Not Solo

Entrepreneurship can sometimes feel like climbing a lonely mountain, but it doesn't have to be that way. One of the smartest moves you can make early on is to create a supportive circle instead of isolating yourself.

Connect with others who are also starting their journeys. They don't necessarily need to be in the same field as you; what truly matters is that you share ambition and honesty.

Start with:

An accountability buddy: someone you can check in with on a weekly basis.

A peer group or community, such as forums, Discord channels, or coworking spaces.

Online creators who inspire you: follow them, learn from them, and engage with their content.

Doing it alone can slow you down and amplify your doubts. But being part of a community can spark momentum, provide clarity, and build resilience. Remember, you're not meant to navigate this path by yourself. Find your tribe and support one another in maintaining the momentum.

Give Back As You Grow

You don't have to wait until you've "made it" to start helping others. Being generous in the early stages can often speed up your growth.

Give back from where you are:

Share the insights you're gaining.

Leave thoughtful comments on someone else's journey.

Respond to a DM with genuine advice.

Post a tip you wish you'd known a year ago.

You don't need money, a substantial following, or fame to create value. All you need is empathy and consistency. Helping others also helps keep your ego in check, your mind open, and your brand rooted in real connections.

Entrepreneurship isn't just about building a business; it's about building people, starting with yourself and then passing that knowledge on.

Legacy in Progress

Take a moment right now. Put everything else aside. Ask yourself:

"What do I want to leave behind, and how can I start making that happen today?"

This question isn't just about crafting a grand legacy; it's about how you show up—today, this week, this year.

Every offer, post, conversation, and interaction with customers contributes to that legacy in real time.

So let's wrap this up with a commitment.

Your Entrepreneur's Promise

I will build boldly.
I will support generously.
I will rise and rest without apology;

I will leave breadcrumbs for those who come after me.

Your story isn't just yours. It's a torch. Pass it on.

Chapter 12: Actionable Tips for a Successful Transition

The Identity Shift- Embracing a New Mindset

Starting your own business isn't just about quitting your job or launching a product—it starts with a mindset shift. As an employee, you followed a roadmap. As an entrepreneur, you create the map. Suddenly, no one tells you what to do next. You set your own deadlines, make your own calls, and carry the weight of your choices.

Letting Go of the Employee Mindset:

Stepping out of the employee mindset means embracing uncertainty:

- Stable paychecks are replaced by calculated risks.
- Clear instructions become self-driven decisions.
- Instead of asking for direction, you start asking yourself, "What's my next move?"

And yes, fear shows up. So does doubt. But these emotions don't mean you're unfit—they mean you're human. The real power lies in walking forward with your values guiding the way, even when fear whispers in the background.

Common Emotional Roadblocks:

Fear of failure: "What if I lose everything?"

Imposter syndrome: “Who am I to do this?”

Comparison trap: “Why is everyone else so ahead?”

The trick isn’t to silence these doubts but to learn to walk alongside them. Entrepreneurship isn’t about being fearless; it’s about moving forward even when you’re scared, with your values ringing louder than your fears.

Set Intentions Like a Visionary (Not Just Goals)

Before you dive into launching a business, take a moment to clarify your “why”- whether it’s freedom, impact, wealth, or creativity. Not every entrepreneur is after the same thing, so it's essential to understand what you’re aiming for.

Define Success on Your Terms:

What do you want your business to provide for you?

How will you measure your success?

Once your intention is clear, break it down into actionable goals.

Short-term goals could include:

- Creating a website
- Identifying three potential clients
- Posting 10 pieces of content

Long-term goals might look like:

- Replacing your salary

- Hiring your first team member
- Expanding into a new market

SMART Goals for Entrepreneurs:

- Specific: "I want to launch a 3-page website by July 1st."
- Measurable: "My goal is to get five paying clients within the next 3 months."
- Achievable: "I'll dedicate 2 hours every weekday after work to this."
- Relevant: "This aligns perfectly with my transition plan."
- Time-bound: "I aim to complete this by Q2."

Momentum builds through clarity. The more defined your goals, the quicker you take action.

Skill Audit: What You Know vs. What You *Need* to Know

You don't have to be perfect. What matters is being honest about your strengths and the areas where you could use some help.

Start with a Skill Audit:

Transferable Skills: Project management, customer service, writing, and budgeting.

Skills to Learn: Marketing, sales, branding, product development.

Don't feel like you need to master everything at once. It's not about becoming an expert; it's about being resourceful.

Build Your Self-Education Plan:

- Read: Atomic Habits (for discipline)
- Listen: How I Built This (for inspiration)
- Join: Online communities where people aren't just flexing—they're helping.

You don't need another degree; what you need is a toolkit and the humility to use it.

Financial Grounding Before You Leap

Nothing derails entrepreneurial dreams faster than financial panic. One of the primary sources of stress for new entrepreneurs is financial instability. Before you take the plunge, be sure to plan.

Understand Your Runway:

- How many months of living expenses do you have saved up?
- Can you cut costs without compromising your well-being?
- Do you have an emergency fund in place?

Side Hustle First, Full-Time Later:

Not every business requires a dramatic moment of quitting your job. Many successful founders started by:

Freelancing on weekends.

Creating digital products while working a 9–5.

Testing services with a small group before scaling up.

A steady transition is still a transition, regardless of its pace. Ensure that you validate your income streams while you have a safety net in place. Security **isn't weakness**—it's wisdom

Basic Budgeting Tips:

From Day one, keep your personal and business expenses separate.

Make it a habit to track your income and expenses every week.

Start planning for taxes early on.

Aim to build a "business buffer" that covers 2–3 months' worth of expenses.

Time Mastery: Stop "Being Busy," Start Being Strategic

Your Calendar Is Your Kingdom—Rule It. You don't need more hours—you need better focus.

Sample Weekly Transition Schedule:

Weekdays

7–8 AM: Focus on skill learning or content planning.

6–9 PM: Dedicate time to client work for your side hustle or building your brand.

Saturday

Set aside 2 hours for deep work without distractions.

Spend 1 hour reviewing and planning for the upcoming week.

Sunday

Take time to rest and recharge (this is essential, not optional).

Remember, your time is an investment. Treat your calendar like a valuable business asset.

Avoiding Burnout:

Schedule in time for rest, meals, and movement.

Set digital boundaries—no more endless scrolling.

Prioritise consistency over intensity (for example, 1 hour daily is better than cramming 8 hours once a week).

You don't need to clock in 40 hours a week to create a future. What you need are focused hours and the discipline to keep showing up for yourself. Protect your time like it's your most valuable asset

Validate Your Idea (Before You Waste Months)

Before investing time, money, and energy in your idea, ensure it addresses a genuine problem. A business doesn't begin with a product—it starts with solving **a problem**.

The Problem–Solution–Fit Approach:

Pinpoint a specific, recurring problem.

Ask yourself: "Who is facing this problem regularly?"

Propose your solution. Does it ease their struggles, save them time or money, or enhance their lives?

Talk to Real People:

Don't go at it alone.

Interview at least 5–10 potential customers. Ask them:

"What's the toughest part about [problem]?"

"What have you tried so far?"

"What would make this easier for you?"

Create feedback loops—test early, test often, and keep it small. A great idea isn't just one you think is brilliant; it's one that people are eager to pay for, recommend, or use regularly.

Market Research Made Simple

You don't need a whole research team—just a curious mind and a few handy free tools.

Find Your Niche:

- Who are you serving?
- What unique need are you addressing?
- What's your unique perspective or twist?

Study Competitors:

- Check out their pricing, content, and customer reviews.

- Ask yourself: What are they doing well? What are they missing?
- Define your edge: faster, friendlier, deeper, more ethical, more personal, etc.

Use Free Research Tools:

- Google Trends to track interest over time.
- Reddit & Quora to discover the questions real people are asking.
- YouTube comments and Amazon reviews for valuable insights.
- Ubersuggest and Answer the Public for keyword exploration.

Research isn't just about data; it's about understanding people on a larger scale. Listen more than you assume.

Product/Service Design

Don't overbuild. Your first version should be just enough to be valuable and testable.

What's an MVP?

Minimum Viable Product = a version of your product that addresses the core problem with minimal features.

Examples:

- A PDF guide instead of an entire course.
- 1:1 coaching calls before launching a group program.
- A pop-up store instead of a full brick-and-mortar location.

Iterative Building Process:

Create → Launch → Collect Feedback

Improve → Relaunch → Repeat

Don't strive for perfection. Strive for momentum. Absolute refinement comes from actual usage, not just brainstorming in a meeting.

Marketing & Sales Strategy

You could have the best offer in the world, but if no one knows about it, it won't matter.

Basic Marketing Channels:

- Organic Content: Blogs, podcasts, social media posts.
- Social Proof: Testimonials, reviews, and screenshots.
- Word of Mouth: Encourage early users to share their experiences.
- Partnerships: Collaborate with others who share your audience.

Crafting Your First Pitch:

Keep it simple. Who are you helping, how do you do it, and why does it matter?

"I assist [target audience] in overcoming [problem] through [your offer]."

For example:

"I assist solopreneurs in landing their first 10 clients using a short-form video strategy."

Creating an Outreach Script:

Hey [Name],

I came across your post about [topic] and thought I'd reach out. I'm currently working on a solution that could be beneficial for you. Would you be open to a chat or sharing some early feedback?

Just keep it genuine, friendly, and not too salesy.

Basic Funding Strategies -Funding: Bootstrapping vs. Going Big

Money Doesn't Grow on Trees (But It Can Grow on Ideas)

Bootstrapping (Self-Funded):

- Fund it yourself (savings, side gigs).
- Pros: Full control. Cons: Slower growth.

This approach is particularly well-suited for service-based businesses, solopreneurs, and digital creators.

External Funding (Using Others' Money):

- Friends & Family: Consider small loans or investments.
- Crowdfunding: Use platforms like Kickstarter or Indiegogo to pre-sell your idea.
- Grants: Search for grants specifically designed for small businesses or innovation.
- Angel Investors/Venture Capital: Ideal for high-growth or tech-focused ideas.

Early-Stage Revenue Ideas:

- Offer a "Founding Member" discount.
- Create a paid waitlist or provide early access.
- Pre-sell a course or product before it's fully developed.

Remember, funding isn't just about cash. It's about maintaining your energy, clarity, and belief in your vision. Choose the path that truly supports you, not just your concept.

Planning & Organisation Tools

A clear mind starts with an organised workspace—both digitally and mentally. These tools can help you organise your thoughts, track your progress, and stay focused.

- **Planning:** Notion (for the organised chaos).
- **Finance:** Wave (free accounting for the frugal).
- **Branding:** Canva (because you're not a designer).
- **Learning:** Coursera (skills > student debt).

Quick Start Tip:

Set up a "Founder Dashboard" that includes:

- Weekly goals

- A long-term vision board

- A task tracker

- An idea dump or journal space

Financial Tools & Templates

Don't let money chaos kill your dream. Make finances a weekly habit.

Helpful Tools:

YNAB – Spend with intention

Wave – Free and simple accounting

QuickBooks – Tax-ready and pro

Spread Sheets – Custom-made for your numbers

Content & Branding Tools

Your story, visuals, and overall presence are crucial. You don't need an entire marketing team to present yourself like a pro.

Go-To Tools:

- Canva: Perfect for creating logos, social media posts, pitch decks, and business cards.

- Grammarly: Helps you write error-free, adjust your tone, and improve clarity.

- Calendly: Makes booking calls a breeze without all the back-and-forth.

Branding Quick Checklist:

- Tone of voice – Is it friendly, expert, playful, or bold?

- Core colours – Choose 2–3 colours that embody your brand's energy.

- Message clarity – Can you sum up what you do in one sentence?

- Consistency – Do your social media, website, and emails all align?

Great branding boils down to clarity, consistency, and connection.

Learning & Growth Resources

Stay curious, but don't get stuck in learning mode

Platforms to Learn:

Coursera – Business leadership and tech form top University-

Skillshare – Bite-sized, creative business classes

YouTube – Free gold mines (try Ali Abdaal)

Must-Subscribe Newsletters:

- Morning Brew – Your go-to for simplified business news.

- The Hustle – Dive into the world of startup culture and gain valuable insights.

- For the Interested – A curated collection of tips for creators and entrepreneurs.

Peer Learning:

Check out communities like Indie Hackers, Elpha (a space for women founders), and- Founder

Your Custom Toolkit:

Every business is unique. Every founder's workflow is different. Choose tools that match your style.

Guided Reflection Prompt:

- How do you prefer to manage tasks: visually, with lists, or on a timeline?

- Do you enjoy using templates, or do you prefer to create your systems?

- Where do you currently feel disorganised?

- What tends to slow you down each week?

- What could make your workload feel lighter?

Action Worksheet: Build Your Startup Stack

- Planning tool: __________

- Finance tracker: __________

- Branding kit: __________

- Learning platform: __________

- Community or peer circle: __________

Keep it straightforward. Start with one tool in each category and let your systems grow in tandem with you.

Your Turn: The Unfiltered Entrepreneur Playbook

1. Identity: Own your new role—you're a founder now.
2. Goals: Dream big, act small (micro-wins matter).
3. Skills: Learn as you go (no one knows it all).
4. Money: Protect your runway like your life depends on it.
5. Time: Be strategic, not just "busy."
6. Validation: Talk to customers *before* you build.
7. Marketing: Sell with story, not spam.
8. Funding: Choose your path (slow & steady or go big).
9. Tools: Use tech, don't drown in it.

10. Mindset: The only failure is quitting.

Now, go and build something that matters.

Verses Kindler Publication

Reach us through our website -

https://www.verseskindlerpublication.com/

For more information visit our

Instagram or Facebook page.